To
Maureen
With Love
Keep being the
awesome Beauty
You are. Making
difference you are
designed by God
to make

Carol
Stanley

BORN TO BE
AWESOME

BORN TO BE Awesome

A Guide to Presenting With Brilliance On Stage Or Camera Through The Power of God In You

CAROL L STANLEY

ELITE

Xulon Press Elite
2301 Lucien Way #415
Maitland, FL 32751
407.339.4217
www.xulonpress.com

Printed in the United States of America.

ISBN-13: 9781545610985

If you are a Christ follower, an entrepreneur, business professional, stage performer, singer, musician, or church leader and want to fulfill your purpose, turn dreams into reality, and become an effective professional communicator through your one-and-only broadcast system—your voice—then read on!

By Carol L. Stanley

TABLE OF CONTENTS

FORWARD

C arol came into my life almost thirty years ago, when I met her during a performance I attended where she spoke and sang. As she shared during that performance, I knew she was a very talented woman with deep passion for enriching others' lives. As our friendship has deepened over the years, God has shown me that Carol was truly *Born to Be Awesome*!

Carol was born with a natural gift to perform. Her magnificent singing ability, her thespian skills, and her unique stage presence placed her before audiences from the time she was just a young child. Also, she was and continues to be beautiful. Can you imagine the accolades she received as she sang and danced in so many venues? It was pretty "heady" for any human being and she loved it. She thought that was to be her life. And it was until, in her late teens, she found the love of her life, married, raised a family, and life showed up. It couldn't be just on stage; it had to be in the trenches of life as well. God wanted to complete His beautiful, perfect little girl who sang and danced, and He did through life and the gift of her giving to others.

Over twenty years ago, Carol wrote her first draft of *Beauty Is an Inside Job*, a book where she introduced the mind map of the tree. When she read it to me, I was "blown away" by the concept, creativity, and ingenuity of her writing. I encouraged her to publish her writing.

However, the reality was it was not God's timing quite yet. Carol was needed in many crisis events happening in her family, and so her deep compassionate need to serve and her God-given strength became her calling during that time.

She went on to develop courses using much of the material and then to be a published author. Only now in *Born to Be Awesome*, is the brilliance of the "Tree of Excellence," her heart, and her life's experiences a published work.

In *Born to Be Awesome,* Carol shares her life stories and life-long experience of teaching and encouraging hundreds of singing students and speaking clients with the skills to not only succeed in their lives, but to thrive! Her unique perspective on the techniques of the use of the voice, as well as the necessary presentation skills, is a gift from God.

Carol is one of God's chosen servants. Take what she has written and learn from it. All the scriptures used throughout the book are the framework of her personal "code of conduct."

Carol has a unique ability to bring the best out in people, and as you read her book, she will accomplish that for you. Her selection of life experiences and scriptural references provide you, the reader, with ready tools you can use in your own life journey.

This book is only the beginning. Carol will go on to give and serve, for that is her persona. She will continue teaching, coaching, writing, and giving presentations. Thousands will be blessed by her many talents and gifts.

I am ninety-eight years old at this writing, and Carol has been a surrogate daughter in Christ. Her love has greatly enriched my life. I hope to live more years to continue to be her mentor.

She has blessed me with this book as we have met weekly over the past year working with all the information. Her thoughts, Biblical truths, and examples in my life to rise above my circumstances in a retirement home have helped me develop a truly optimistic and useful pattern in all I do. She has shown me the importance of being aware of my thoughts and choices in how I choose to think and speak. I have used the information and put it to work in my life. At ninety-eight I have a mind that is sharp and keen, am optimistic in spirit, and I love serving Jesus! Carol has blessed me and she will bless you. Read on because *Born to Be Awesome* will change your life!

Chaplain Alma Gray Martin

DEDICATION

I dedicate this book to my precious mother, Edna Earle Ware Hunnicutt, and my precious and gifted father, Clyde Jefferson Hunnicutt, Jr.

It is because of their love, talents, gifting, and belief in me that I am sharing this book, my heart on paper, with you. They both passed at the close of 2014 within six weeks of each other, Mother on October twentieth at age ninety-two, and Dad on December third, two weeks short of age ninety-seven.

For the past sixteen plus years of my life I have cared for them. I flew to Phoenix every three months for several years, then every month, and finally every two weeks as their needs grew. I helped them through the emotional difficulty of moving out of their home of fifty years in Phoenix to the Seattle area to live with my husband and me, the devastation of Mother's Alzheimer's disease and the toll it takes on a family, and Daddy's struggle through it all. But my prayer has always been to help them finish well and go home to heaven together where absolute healing resides.

God has been faithful to answer my prayer and allow me to experience both Mother and Daddy accepting and believing in Jesus for real. I had the privilege of holding Daddy's hand and praying with him as he became honest before the Lord and accepted the free gift of eternal life from Jesus. I also had the honor of being with him as he took his last breath and joined Mother. They now are home together with Jesus and eternally healthy and whole in the light of His presence.

I will be eternally grateful for the experience of caring for Mother and Daddy for those years and all the joy and beauty in my life they provided. I am also thankful for all the trials of those years, as they have helped me to become a new person. I am a better "me" because of God's faithfulness and love through it all. My parents have always been a blessing to me. I am part of them and they are part of me. My dedication and thankfulness to God for them is deep and profound.

ACKNOWLEDGMENTS

There are so many to thank for encouragement and support. My husband, Mike, is the first on my list. He has lovingly endured all the time I spent writing at home and away on our getaway trips for our fiftieth wedding anniversary year of 2014, and beyond. He has been a great encourager to me, always assuring me that what I am doing is important, and that means a great deal to me.

I owe a great deal of thanks to all of my students and clients who have encouraged me to put my teaching, coaching techniques, and philosophy in a book for all to see and experience. Their encouragement has been well appreciated. My prayer is that this work will continue to bless them and others.

A special thanks to Alma Gray-Martin, who has been my biggest support and encourager. She met with me on a regular basis to go over my manuscript with suggestions and encouragement. It has meant so much to me to have her ever-faithful support all through the writing process, good days and doubting days. Alma has been a fabulous mentor to me. My hope is for everyone to experience the privilege of having a mentor, and to be a mentor to others. There is great power in mentorship and a huge blessing for everyone involved in it.

A big thank you to Peter McKinnon, who took my simple graphics of the "Tree of Excellence," stool, and soldier, and turned them into brilliant graphics. Thank you, Peter. He can be reached at: McKinnon Design, LLC, http://www.mckinnondesign.com, and http://www.freelock.com.

A huge thank you to my endorsers of this work. My life work is wrapped up, in part, in this book, and it means a lot to me to have their support and encouragement.

I also owe a great deal of thanks to Dr. Caroline Leaf for all her fabulous work with the brain, mind, body, and spirit. Her books have truly inspired me to apply some of her research data in this book. I encourage all who read this book to read all her works. You will truly be blessed by them.[1,2]

Dr. Ken Keis of Consulting Resource Group Leader of Canada has been very helpful with his understanding of all the aspects of the psychology of personality. All my years of being trained in personality came to new light with the help of CRG leader and Ken. He offers great training at CRGleader.com in Canada on this very interesting and important subject matter and related topics, and I recommend them highly.[5]

Thank you to Cheri Tree and all the team at BANKcode. com. Cheri's brilliant creation and scientific endorsement of her work with the white paper from San Francisco State University has blessed me as a BANKcode certified and licensed trainer. All her work and new book, *Why They Buy,* are blessing many others around the world to understand the power of these unique values in relationships of all kinds, buying behavior, and business sales.[6]

Thank you to my Pastor, Dan Larson, and his lovely wife, Diane. They have believed in me and have encouraged me greatly to continue to use my gifts and talents to bless others. In Scripture there is no such thing as "retirement," as far as I can see. I think God wants us to be viable and useful to bless others until He chooses to take us home to heaven. I deeply appreciate their love and faithfulness to me, my husband, Mike, and the other members of Family Life Community Church, where we are all loved and valued.

Endorsements:

"Anything that Carol Stanley touches has a touch of excellence and class. This book is no exception! In reading it, I can feel her passion, hear her heart, and glean from years of wisdom and experience. I recommend this book to anyone wanting to take their professional or personal life to the "next level." You won't be disappointed."
—Pastors Dan and Diane Larson, Family Life Community Church

"Carol taught me more about how to use my voice in one hour than I have learned in a lifetime. Her knowledgeable and compassionate teaching style made me feel comfortable immediately. (Pretty important when you're already nervous about using your voice in the first place!) Thank you, Carol, from the bottom of my heart. You have truly helped me learn how to use MY voice." —Jamie W

"I can't say enough good things about the workshop and the private coaching that I have received from Carol Stanley. My voice is stronger now and I feel more confident, even at that critical first second on the stage. Something about Carol's enveloping warmth and encouragement stays with me. THANK YOU, Carol!"
—Katie M

"In working with Carol, I have learned to be aware of my thoughts and choices in how I think and speak. She has blessed me with her knowledge and practical truths that have transformed me at ninety-eight to be even more effective in my chaplain work at this awesome age!"
—Alma M

"Carol has been a fantastic voice teacher, stage director, and coach for me. She helped me gain the skills and confidence to do high soprano solos and gutsy alto range parts with ease in my musical comedy career. She is amazing!"
—Cathy B

"Carol has helped me so much with this recent campaign. She has shown me the importance and power of authentic delivery. Her warm, yet "get the job done," attitude has really helped me improve my public speaking so much."
—Linda K, political candidate and public servant

"Finding our purpose for being, increasing our leadership skills, and defining a clear mission statement have been a challenge until Carol's training on Life of Purpose. We now have a much better handle on who we are and where we are going, thanks to Carol."
—FLCC Church Interns

"Carol, it is great to see you are still helping others. I attended one of your seminars a couple years ago, and I remember a lot of excellent content."
—Thomas G

"Carol's 'Rock the Stage with Spirit, Body, Soul and Big Impact Workshop' focused our group on the important elements of praise

and worship; from audience engagement to vocal skills to physically showing up at our best."　　—Doxa Church Worship Team

"Wow! Carol has helped me so much in my marriage, and parenting
skills. Relationship mastery with personality understanding, and her
warm effective mentoring have been key for me." —Anonymous

"I have used Carol Stanley for several years now getting help with
my presentations. Thank you, Carol Stanley. I love working with
you and am blessed by your friendship and support. I have enjoyed
working with you on my speaking and presentations. Wow, what a
mind map you developed for me. It is wonderful. It is so wonderful
to work with you!!!"　　　　　　　　　　　　　　—Diane N

INTRODUCTION

M ost people write books that are guides to a certain number of steps to be of help to you in whatever the subject matter. What you will see with this book is that it is a guide for sure. But it is more than a simple few steps guide. Excellence in voice and presentation require a vast understanding of not only the vocal systems, but so much more.

You will discover that you are a triune person. As such, you need a full understanding of who you are, Whose you are, your purpose, the keys of knowing your spirit, mind, and body, your vocal systems, professional image, your personality, the power of presence, and so much more for you to truly "shine and present with brilliance."

Communication and speaking are issues we all must deal with no matter if we are on a stage or just sharing with one or more friends at a party or networking group. In the same way, effective communication with your spouse and family requires the same knowledge. I have observed singers who may sing relatively well but have no clue as to what it takes to speak well, and certainly vice versa.

After more than forty years of training people in these skills of singing and speaking, I have seen singers do well, yet not always connect the dots to their speaking skills. You must understand that speaking and singing require the same knowledge and skill sets. The singer simply takes the vocal skills to a greater level, but all the rest is the same.

Research from US population phobias states that sixty-eight percent of people are phobic and fearful of death. But even more, at seventy-four percent, are phobic and fearful of public speaking. There are solutions to these problems, and this book will provide them for you.

My hope and prayer for you is that this book will enlighten you and give you *hope and a future* beyond your wildest dreams, enabling you to be the *Awesome* person God created you to be, and fulfill all your dreams and goals of speaking or singing and presenting your message brilliantly.

Chapter 1

WHY THIS BOOK, WHY NOW?

"Yes, indeed—God is my salvation. I trust, I won't be afraid. God—yes God!—is my strength and song, best of all, my salvation!"

—Isaiah 12:2, (MSG)

Vocal Application*: You must understand the full implication of who you are, what your voice really is, and that it all is important to your success in life. God has called each of you to a unique purpose and plan for the life He has given you. All of you, the whole you, is wrapped up in your voice. You are your voice and your voice is you. Your strength and song in your heart depend on your trust in God. Don't ever let questions about yourself or God stop you. Rather, let them start you on a pursuit and discovery of answers to knowing*

yourself, your significance, and God better. The Word of God is full of answers to who He is, to who you are, and why you exist. Doesn't it make sense to know and trust the God who created you and who created the universe, rather than trusting the universe, as so many do today? The universe truly has no power—only God has and is the power you need to be all He has created you to be, do, and have. "And my God will supply all your needs according to His riches in glory in Christ Jesus."
—**Philippians 4:19 (NASB)**

This book is meant to encourage you. Identity and personal significance are key to transformation, and this book is all about your transformation into a confident presenter. You are *fearfully and wonderfully* created with greatness inside you. That greatness exists so you can share it with others to bless them and you. They are waiting for you to bring forth your unique specialness so that they may hear, see, interact with, and be inspired by you. You can effectively deliver all you have to give through your business, your church, your community, your home, and, indeed, all aspects of your life.

- Have you ever thought voice study was for singers only?
- Have you ever thought that if you were not a singer, or weren't interested in being a singer, that the study of voice was not important or pertinent to your success?
- Have you ever really thought about how the real you expresses itself?

The truth is that the God-given, authentic you can only be released for others to see, feel, and experience through your physical presence and, more importantly, the broadcast system of the human voice. Your voice encompasses your total demeanor and is an important asset to your success.

Have you ever wanted a second chance to make a great first impression, whether it be how you physically presented yourself in your appearance, or whether it was what you said and the way you said it, or all the above?

I think we all have had that experience of wanting another "shot" at presenting a better picture of us at one time or another. I have been coaching and training people to be their best for more than forty years. One of my specialties is training singers in vocal and performance skills, and all of them display the desire to do better next time.

People have been asking me to write down my teaching methods for years, so finally, I am doing it. I've always known that voice was not for singers only. But it was at a special business meeting when the awesome reality that voice is not just for singers hit me in a **new** way. Voice is for many other vocal circumstances and venues as well.

May I Please Do Over?

I was experiencing a "wish I had a do-over" moment. When I arrived I was tired after working hard all day on my marketing material for the meeting. I came in late, felt rushed, had to immediately present myself and my business, and couldn't pull my best self together in time. I felt like I royally "blew" my sixty-second presentation of what I do. Can you relate? For most of the people in the room, I'm sure it wasn't as bad as I felt it was, but what bothered me was I knew it wasn't my best me.

As a consummate professional voice artist and trainer on many levels of expertise, I subconsciously thought I should never have those moments, or should somehow be exempt from those moments. So I thought!

I felt a bit "shot down," but after I prayed and asked God to help me focus on who I really am and my mission, and as the evening's festivities kept progressing, I refocused, stayed involved, and gave of myself to help where I could.

After the dinner meal was served and consumed, I felt a bit better. A time came in the program where we were to share something that we were donating for a raffle to benefit the organization's non-profit foundation. Just before it was my turn to share, the microphone went out—it stopped working. This was a serendipitous moment put there, I believe by God, to show me something in a new way.

I now felt in my power as a professional actor/singer. I was experiencing the real me, the authentic God-given me who cared deeply about these women, men, and the organization. I wanted the best for all of them, and to experience the gift of my training that I was donating. I was not the "tired, hurried, worried about what I was going to say" person from a few hours before. What I had to give was from my heart, the very depth of my being. It came from love and truth deep within me. What came out of me was a strong, commanding, authentically loving, caring, and excited me expressed through my now better-connected instrument—my "real me" voice—the one I knew as a singer. The microphone was totally unnecessary in that large room, even if it had been working, because of the power and control of my God-given voice, which added to the impact of the gift of training I was offering.

As I concluded the evening, it dawned on me, with a whole new awareness, that all the people in that room (including me, the professional) needed the unique training, understanding, and focus I had to offer them whether they were singers or not. It became clearer than ever to me that we can all get caught up in being "taken out" of our true self and "blow" the expression of ourselves and our message. We can "blow" the expression of who we are and what we have to offer this world, no matter how good we think we are, or how exempt we think we are from failure to focus on vital life and vocal truths. We all need insurance for those moments. We all need coping awareness, and new skills that assure us of success in any moment of communication, but especially public ones.

I realized that viewing voice training **only** for singers or actors was terribly narrow and short-sided. I knew what to do as a singer/ performer in a musical or stage situation, but this speaking engagement made me painfully aware that I needed to use **all** I knew about vocal awareness and focus **all** the time when speaking or singing. The deep ministering work of the total God-given connection of the spirit, mind, and body that is true for singers is desperately needed and just as true and important for anyone speaking anything to anybody, anywhere, anytime. It was truly a special AHA moment for me!

I have been blessed to work with many great vocal trainers who understand the vocal mechanism as a more physical and/or mental entity. There is so much to be learned and appreciated there, and I am deeply grateful for all the insights I have gained as a student myself. But there is much more. All my training—coupled with much professional experience as a singer, recording and concert artist, model, actress, stage and choral director, and voice and performance skills trainer, as well as an ongoing long-term relationship with God and His inspired Word, the Bible—has shown me that voice is so much more than something physical or mental. So, what does that all mean?

Voice is truly the expression of the deeper God-given whole you, including all aspects of your spirit, mind and body.

In order to understand and to be able to access the deeper whole you, you must be inspired and empowered to get in touch with and experience the physical side of voice and all that entails. You must also be in touch with and master the intellectual, emotional, and willful focus of the mental side of voice. Finally, you must get in touch with and experience the connective gift of you that is unique to the spiritual side of voice. God uniquely enables you to be amazingly effective as you give the gift of yourself to others. This is where the real you shines forth and where all the fun and payback exist for all your hard work. It is a lot like the line from the movie, *Chariots of Fire*. When the main character was asked why he ran as a track athlete in the Olympics, when he could be on the mission field serving God in the way perceived by others to be correct for him, he said, "Because, I feel God's pleasure when I run."

Why Do You Want to Speak or Sing?

Just like the gentleman runner in the movie, *Chariots of Fire,* I want you to feel God's pleasure in you as you speak or sing. My desire is that you be free to be the beautiful, whole, authentic, and real **you**, beautifully expressing yourself through the awesome broadcast system God created—your own human voice.

You will feel His pleasure as you speak and purposefully do what you were designed by Him to be and do.

Why Me?

[handwritten: I want to communicate to the world the importance of talking about SOL wished so everyone can get involved experience peace when end of life comes.]

One of the first few questions I ask a new student or client is, "Why are you here? Why do you want to speak or sing?" The reason I ask these questions is they make you think and dig for the answers. Hopefully, your answers will begin to open you up to the **why me** in your life and all the possibilities in this book.

I am passionate about reaching out and helping you to be your very best in all the areas in which you desire to improve. It may be in business, or it may be in your personal life. I have access to some fabulous keys to unlock the real you and free you to explore and find your true self, true loves, and passions for the life you've been given. For these are where your unique messages will emerge.

What this book and the content of all my coaching and voice training is about is freeing you to be, and continue to be, the best **you** anytime, anywhere, with anyone. Attaining that kind of freedom will empower you to feel God's pleasure in you, as you effectively deliver the power of God in you through your God-given message, whether it be a business meeting, an interview, public speaking message, or song or recording session. And I can't wait to get started!

Chapter 2

WOULD THE REAL ME PLEASE STAND UP!

"For you created my inmost being; you knit me together in my mother's womb. I praise you because I am fearfully and wonderfully made; your works are wonderful, I know that full well."
—**Psalms 139:13–14,** (NIV)

Vocal Application: *You must know who you are and that you are unique and special with specific gifts to share. Speaking and singing are the best form of total communication because your voice, your one-and-only broadcast system, encompasses all of you, spirit, mind, and body—the real triune whole you. Your voice encompasses the physical voice, body language, thoughts, intent, and the ability to hear from your Maker at any given point in time. All of you communicates to others. The "sweet spot"* *of your voice comes forth as you understand the physiology and science of voice and presentation, and truly knowing yourself, which we will discuss further in a later chapter. You must know you are very significant and allow your significance to show through by being your "excellent" best.*

Over the years, I have met and worked with so many people who truly do not know who they really are. Not knowing who you are hampers you in so many ways, one of which is not knowing your purpose in life. I will share about your purpose in a later chapter. My heart truly goes out to you because you are missing a whole wonderful dimension of life by not being clear as to **who** you are, **Whose** you are, and a sense of your destiny. If unclear about these things, you are missing and not understanding your powerful significance.

So, Who Are You?

I bet you think you are the daughter or son of your mom and dad, brother or sister to your siblings, aunt or uncle to nieces and nephews, wife or husband to your mate, parent to children, grandparent to your grandchildren; or who you are as a business owner, employee, or career person. It is very common to identify with your family positions or what you do when asked who you are. So, given the list above, take a moment to determine whom you identify with when asked who you are.

I am a child of God, a person of Integrity and compassion who's values are relationships, honor family unity, respect and a whole lot of humor!

To really answer the question of who you are, I must refer to the One who actually created you. In my favorite compilation of books called the Holy Bible, in a book called Psalms, in the chapter numbered one hundred thirty nine, in the verse numbered fourteen (Psalms 139:14), God Himself tells you that you are *"fearfully and wonderfully made."* But more than that, He tells you in the whole chapter how He knows you intimately, because He knows everything about you even before you were born. And His thoughts are precious toward you. In other words, He created you and loves you.

Wow! That soothes a deep place in me to know that the Creator of the universe created me, knows me, loves me deeply, and "has my back!"

God also tells you and me in a book called Ephesians,

> *"Even before he made the world, God loved [you]*
> *and chose [you] in Christ to be holy and without*
> *fault in His eyes."* —Ephesians 1:4, (NLT).

He sees you and me without fault! I love that, because I know I am not always faultless. Who isn't encouraged to know God sees you perfect and faultless as He created you to be? In fact, Graham Cook, a wonderful Bible teacher says that his definition of grace is simply choosing to live daily step by step by how God sees you; He sees you as perfect, faultless, and totally able to fulfill His divine purpose for you and your life. That is an awesome thought that takes the pressure off of trying to be good enough for God and others. He already sees you as His perfect child because of His grace toward you.

11

Now, I know I am human and therefore carry elements of the human nature that automatically separates me from God, even though He sees me without fault. I know I am not perfect and need a way to be united with God through a Savior, as do all of us. But God gave every person a way to reconnect to God the Father through Jesus, His Son. That is an amazing gift, to be able to accept the free gift of Jesus as Savior through the gift of choice to believe, get to know Jesus personally through His Word the Bible, and thereby be totally reconnected to God.

You and I, as humans, seem to love rules. As a result, we have created many denominations and complicated sets of rules. But God is all about relationship, and He created us as human "beings" to hang out with Him, rather than being caught up in human "doings" that only create extra rules and make us too busy to hear and experience Him. Religion is all about rules and ways to get to God by our behavior or performance. God is saying, "No need for your rule making. I gave you a few, ten to be exact, for your own good, which provide you with structure and happiness. Now I am giving you my Son as a gift so you can truly experience Me and all I have for you. This is a gift you only need to accept by faith. Believe with all your heart that I love you and want your excellent best for you always."

"I am the Way, the Truth and the Life. No one can come to the Father except through Me." —John 14:6, (NLT).

Jesus tells us He is the only way to truly be reconciled and connected to Father God. The whole book of John is so awesome

12

because it is a love letter explicitly written to you. In fact, the whole Bible is a love letter, because it points you to Jesus, in whom you can find freedom, acceptance, love, and purpose.

The Bible is full of other references that declare God's love for you. The point is, you are awesome! Not because I say so, but because God says so, and you can trust Him above anyone or anything on this planet. I believe that accepting this gift of Jesus as Savior allows you to see that God sees you as perfect and totally forgiven. Knowing that allows you to live your life learning to forgive yourself and live into your perfectness and grace in His eyes.

So, who are you? Do you know the incredible you, and the unique purpose He has given you? Perhaps it will help you begin to find yourself by my sharing a bit of who I am.

Carol's Story

You now know that I, like you, am a child of God, created by God and loved. And I now know He has my back, and has a unique plan for my life as He does for you. My unique purpose plan has been coming to life for years and is, in fact, why I am writing this book. It all started when I became aware of the spark within me of loving to perform for others.

I was the kid creating games to play with my friends and deciding how they should be played. Have you ever created a backyard play with sheets on the clothesline for your curtains and had your friends help be the actors, and/or the audience? Most of my friends wanted to just be the audience, but a few brave ones wanted to be on stage and join me in the acting part. I loved directing the process, and I was only ten years old! Before that I had danced and sung on local TV shows, and in many recitals.

At age thirteen, while attending a church service in the little church near my home, I experienced the incredibly strong voice and pull of the Holy Spirit of God tugging me forward to choose to believe and accept the gift of eternal salvation with Jesus as my personal Savior. That powerful tug of the Holy Spirit was stronger than any stage fright or anything else I had experienced before. My pride created fear and I resisted going forward publicly. But I finally succumbed, went forward, and proclaimed my belief and choice to follow Jesus in my life. It was my "baby beginning" with Jesus.

I loved singing solos in church. One of my mother's, grand-mother's, and my favorites was "You'll Never Walk Alone" from the Broadway show, *Carousel*. I was drawn, even then, to singing different kinds of music with special meaning in church to honor God and help others see Him in the message of the music.

In high school, I was honored to be accepted into Arizona All State choral performance groups and other specialized performing groups, musicals, dramas, etc. I had some amazing directors who shaped my love for pulling the best out of people, as they did in me. I fell in love with how that felt. There I also experienced some "not so great" music teachers. I truly wanted to "rid the world" of bad music teachers by being the best I could possibly be, and by teaching and helping others to be their best also. So how is that for an arrogant eighteen-year-old attitude!

Then in college, even as a freshman, I had the opportunity to direct our college concert choral groups several times (concert choir and madrigals a-cappella choir). That was an amazing soul-touching realization of just how much I truly loved the challenge of verbally painting pictures for these choirs in order to bring their best out through music.

As a young artist, I knew I loved performing, but I also knew that I loved teaching and pulling great things out of others. Having a family was of even greater importance to me—a family like the one I grew up in, strong, loving, and highly valued. So I had a serious decision to make when I was proposed to by my husband of now over fifty years. I chose what I believe was the God-ordained path of husband and family for me as a priority.

Even though having chosen a family life, I still had a tremendous desire for performing and being my best. So I kept my education going as a young wife and mother, and kept performing at churches and concerts, and recording professionally.

I saw myself performing at Carnegie Hall, which represented the epitome of excellence to me, and influencing many people. Even though I never got to Carnegie, I kept acting in local Broadway musicals as lead actress, and perfecting my craft by using excellence within it. As part of my ongoing education and training I was blessed to work with great performers and excellent trainers, Marni Nixon of Hollywood and movie fame, being one of my favorites. I began professional modeling, and eventually I went on to teach others those skills as well.

I was pursued to direct a choral group for young mothers and to teach voice to them and many others. One of the things that was so fun for those ten years of directing that group, was seeing those wives and mothers grow and become great stage performers with costuming, staging, choreography, and the works. They were no longer just a choral group of ordinary wives and moms, but a true performance troupe performing to sold-out crowds at the

Play House in Seattle's World fair site called Seattle Center. What happened to their confidence and image of self was truly amazing. They began truly believing in who they were as God-created individuals with gifts, talents, and desires to be more. This actually allowed them to bring more to their families because they were more centered and deeply fulfilled inside themselves. They discovered they had significance, and that led them to the excellence I required of them.

I have always been a believer in "having your cake and eating it, too!" So, because being a great wife and mother was important to me, I wanted to protect their marriages and families as well. I made sure our rehearsals always had quality childcare just down the hall from us in the rehearsal hall, and that we rehearsed in the daytime so as not to interfere with family time. We did have our "cake" and did "get to eat it also." As a performer and director, I kept using and honing my craft.

Creating and performing my own concerts allowed me to hone the skills as a solo concert artist while I directed my band and back-up singers. It also gave me the opportunity to develop special lighting effects and learn how to set lights. During that time I created a special concert to take to Israel, complete with singers and band.

I have been the prime vocal teacher and coach for many individuals and performance and worship groups. It was great fun to set blocking and run lighting at the Seattle Fifth Avenue Theater for a prominent church group, of which I was the voice trainer and coach for their lead singers. I had the privilege of being in several movies shot in Seattle. I hosted and currently host my own radio show, and I have performed and been interviewed on countless TV shows. I have recorded music albums and continue to help others understand the ins and outs and skills of the recording process. And directing actors and singers on stage, as well as private coaching, continues to be a great source of joy to me.

I have seen great transformation in those I have worked with for many years. It is my passion and purpose to help lift you up as you climb in your career. The joy of "performance" (meaning doing your best) and "entertainment" (meaning inviting others in with you) is ever present in me, but the joy of seeing you achieve and become your best is even greater in me now.

All this sharing of my past is not to boast, but to demonstrate that God is in control and He will make sure you have the experiences you need to become the best representative of Himself as you fulfill your God-given purpose. You will always feel His pleasure when you pursue what you were uniquely designed for. My design and purpose is to help others with the insights from all the experiences He has allowed and ordained in my life, the good and bad ones, the happy easy ones, and the unhappy difficult ones. We all have a choice to be bitter or better with what we experience. I choose better, for sure, and want you to do so as well.

I believe that "Beauty is an Inside Job" (copyrighted title of one of my courses), and that all you go through helps shape the true beauty in you as a gift to give away to others, whether through music, speaking to groups, or building one-on-one relationships in your personal or business life. We all have something to say of importance to others, no matter what profession or business it is, whether you are a public speaker or singer or not. We all have a voice to be used for good, and using it will bring you and others joy when used to bring the gift of you to bless them.

Chapter 3

THE "TREE OF EXCELLENCE" SAYS IT ALL

"Blessed are those who trust in the Lord and have made the Lord their hope and confidence. They are like trees planted along a riverbank, with roots that reach deep in the water. Such trees are not bothered by the heat or worried by long months of drought. Their leaves stay green, and they never stop producing fruit." **—Jeremiah 17:7–8,** (NLT)

Vocal application: *You are designed to be effective as a gifted speaker and singer no matter what you may experience in your life. In fact, only life can teach you gems to be spoken and shared. Your ultimate confidence comes from knowing you are a child of God, gifted by God to take your message to the world around you. It takes relying on and trusting God to be effective in all your relationships with Him,* *yourself, and others. It takes all your assets and appropriate spiritual, mental, and physical nourishment to assure your fruit bearing, or productiveness, as you speak and sing well. You really are more like a tree than you may have thought.*

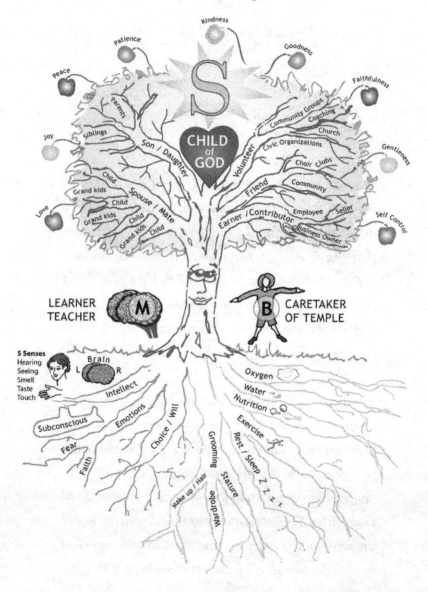

S cripture says you are like a tree. I call it the "**Tree of Excellence.**"

> *"Blessed is the one who does not walk in step with*
> *the wicked or stand in the way that sinners take or*
> *sit in the company of mockers, but whose delight is*
> *in the law of the LORD, and who meditates on his law*
> *day and night. **That person is like a tree planted by***
> ***streams of water, which yields its fruit in season***
> ***and whose leaf does not wither—whatever they do***
> ***prospers."*** —Psalms 1:1–3, (NIV)

So the Bible tells you that you are like a tree planted by water that bears fruit constantly with leaves that never wither. That is pretty powerful. You are like a tree with your leaves always green, bearing fruit constantly, and **all** you do will prosper. Wow! Another awesome promise from God to you. That means that no matter the season of life you are in, you are always "green" with shade for others and always productive with fruit for them as well.

So what does the "Tree of Excellence" have to do with voice? You are like a tree and your voice is expressed through your spirit (you are a child of God), mind (you are a learner and teacher), and body (you are the caretaker of your temple). The tree represents you and expresses your roles in life.

The "Tree of Excellence" is a great visual to help you see the important connection between your spirit, mind, and body, the whole you, and thus, your voice. God imparted this image to me in my mind as I was praying years ago, and it thrilled me to discover it was all there in Scripture.

What does a tree need to sprout, grow, and thrive? My husband, Mike, is a master gardener and has helped me to see even more clearly how a tree sprouts, grows, and what it needs to thrive. I am fascinated by the tree and how much, like you and me, the tree analogy really shows.

A tree first needs a place to be planted or anchored. The seed needs soil (nutrients), moisture, sunlight, and temperature (degree of warmth) to sprout or "die to itself," shed its seed life, and be reborn into a plant that can begin to grow.

Many seeds are planted below the surface of the soil, where they shed their seed skins and begin to come to life in the wet and warm soil, sending a root down, and then a seed leaf that pops up reaching for the light. Some seeds don't get planted below the surface of the soil and only need the light, temperature, and moisture to begin to grow, like many tree seeds that just fall to the ground and manage to sprout a root down and seed leaf up. The root anchors the plant in the soil, and then the root can begin to look for nutrients that will feed the new plant. The sprouting leaves use warmth and energy from the sun to continue to energize the roots, and the roots feed nutrients back to the leaves. The plant now forms a stem, and then the real leaves of the tree begin to develop. As the tree grows, it needs more and more water, sun, warmth, or temperature appropriate to the species, and nutrients from the soil to keep the cycle going.

Now, let's look at this from a perspective of humanity. You need water, warmth, sunshine, nutrition, and a good soil in which to be planted and anchored, like a safe home environment.

Look at the tree again at the beginning of this chapter. It has roots, trunk, branches, leaves, and, if healthy, has fruit. A tree must be planted in good soil so its roots have access to water and nutrients so as to carry them up to the tree's leaves. It also must have full spectrum sunlight to perform the miracle of photosynthesis, which transforms those nutrients and water into life-giving energy and ultimately blossoms and fruit.

You are like that tree in that you must be anchored in life, and you have two distinct root systems of nutrient intake, your body and mind (which incorporates the brain). You also have a complete tree top with evergreen leaves for shade-giving and fruit of the Spirit. You are a triune multi-sensory being (spirit—child of God, mind—learner/teacher, body—caretaker of your temple).

What you taste, smell, drink, or consume feeds your body. You are the caretaker of the temple of the Holy Spirit, your body.

What you see (read and watch), hear (listen to), smell, touch, taste, and feel feeds your mind. You are a learner and teacher as a caretaker of your mind root area, and a choice maker.

Your root branches of body and mind below ground represent your relationship with yourself and must be monitored closely.

The top of your tree is representative of your spirit area. You are a child of God. You can only take in full spectrum sunlight by connecting to God's Spirit, and those fulfilling sunshine moments in life were designed for you to experience total health as a gift from Him. You can grow without God, but it is like growing a tree in artificial light. It grows but does not produce healthy robust fruit.

The miracle of "Son-light" (having Jesus in your heart as your best friend) truly allows you to experience the full spectrum spiritual sunlight benefits in life. There are great testimonies of countless people who have been transformed in a life-giving way by accepting Jesus in their lives and developing a personal relationship with Him, thus wanting to do good for others.

The top of the tree is about the branches and leaves where miraculous energy exchange takes place and ultimately fruit is produced. These branches represent relationships in life with God and others. You have three major types of branches: earner/contributor, volunteer/friend, and family (child, sibling, mate, parent, aunt or uncle, grandparent).

Your branches of career, employment, business ownership, and money sustaining endeavors all relate to communication with other people in those areas of life. You are an earner/contributor as an employee or business owner, a provider for your family, and a generous giver to worthwhile causes.

Your branches of volunteerism and friendship relate to people at church, in civic groups, and in your community activities. You are a volunteer, friend, and productive community member.

And you have family branches, all of which represent people you must relate to and communicate with—difficult or not. You are a child of your parents, sibling to your brothers and/or sisters, aunt or uncle to your nieces and nephews, mate to your spouse, parent to your children if God has blessed you with them, and grandparent if you are blessed to have them.

The amount of fruit on your tree directly represents the fruit of the Spirit of God that you demonstrate in your relationships: love, joy, peace, patience, kindness, goodness, faithfulness, gentleness, and self-control. I don't know about you, but I need miraculous help to pull off exhibiting all that fruit in **all** my relationships. Without God's kind of "agape" unconditional love and forgiveness, relationships can be disasters. I need to have the "power plug" of my life plugged into the power source of God's Spirit in order to exhibit healthy relationships with all their joys and challenges.

You and I need the fruit of God's Spirit in all areas of our lives. As a speaker you must understand the power and importance of who you are as a brilliant, thriving, productive "Tree of Excellence" connected to the power source of God. It is in the connection to "Son-light" and the pollinators of positive people in your life that you are able to produce comforting shade and good fruit to nourish others through your demeanor and message. The benefit to your audience is huge, as God is fueling the gifts in you to bless others through your speaking or singing.

In the Biblical book of John, chapter fifteen, Jesus tells us He is the vine and you are the branches. We usually read that to mean He is the vine and all of us as humans are the branches. But I want to suggest a new view, that Jesus is your core vine or trunk of your tree, deeply integrated into the very bark and internal fiber of your tree trunk, and that the rest of you are the root branches and treetop branches that are connected to Him, your trunk. Jesus goes on to say you can do nothing without Him. He chose you to stay connected and produce great and wonderful fruit to nourish others.

Chapter 4

JESUS IS REAL

"Don't let your hearts be troubled. Trust in God, and trust also in Me. There is more than enough room in my Father's home. If this were not so, would I have told you that I am going to prepare a place for you? When everything is ready, I will come and get you, so that you will always be with me where I am. And you know the way to where I am going."

"No, we don't know, Lord," Thomas said. "We have no idea where you are going, so how can we know the way?"

Jesus told him, "I am the way, the truth, and the life. No one can come to the Father except through me." —**John 14:1–6,** (NLT)

Vocal Application: *Many don't believe in Jesus and don't "get" who He is—not unlike Thomas, who did not know where Jesus was going. Speaking and singing require you to be able to deal with people and relationships in healthy ways. The fruit of God's Spirit and the shade of forgiveness are critical in doing this. Jesus and the Holy Spirit of God give you the insight and help needed to grow fruit, create inspiring messages, and be able to deliver them well. He is real, and the "magic bullet" is knowing Him, who you are, why you are here, what you are to do in life, and your success in all areas of your life. You cannot speak or sing inspirationally, motivationally, or effectively without Him. Remember to: "Take delight in the Lord and He will give you the desires of your heart"* **—Psalms 37:4,** (NIV)

When people speak of the "law of attraction," they are tuning into the power of operation in the fruit of God's Spirit. Love, joy, peace, patience, kindness, goodness, faithfulness, gentleness, and self-control will always attract others to you. Your energy will always resonate high, as that is the way God designed you to resonate, with His fruit so that you become the "light of the world" as He is and said you would be.

When I am in relationships daily with others, I need help to deal with people. That help only comes from God Himself, by knowing the person of Jesus. I have not always experienced the benefits of truly knowing Jesus. I knew about Him, went to church, prayed, even accepted His gift of salvation at age thirteen. But it was not until I was in my late twenties that I really fell to my knees and realized that I needed to totally "sell out" to Jesus. All I can say is He unmistakably met me where I was when I looked up to heaven in frustration and asked Him (yelled actually) if He was real. He delivered. I became a new woman inside and I knew it.

As stated before, when I was thirteen years old and singing in church, I admitted I needed Jesus and chose to accept Jesus' loving offer of salvation and was baptized in the church baptismal water tank. I will never forget the huge discomfort I felt as the Holy Spirit was tugging at my heart to yield. I argued and finally said, "Uncle," and went forward to publicly say "yes" to God and accept His gracious offer of eternal life.

After that He was always with me, but I never got to really **know** Him until I committed my life in a new and meaningful way in my late twenties after giving birth to three of my four children. I remember starting to doubt my belief as all my performing and cultural influences tried to pull me away from my faith in Him. Yet I remembered the light of Truth that I felt as that thirteen-year-old when I first yielded to the strong pull of the Holy Spirit to go forward and trust in Jesus. That pull was stronger than anything I had ever experienced. No performance nerves or anything else could match the Holy Spirit's pull when He called!

As a twenty-eight-year-old, I remember getting down on my knees and asking Jesus if He was real, and if so, to show me. And He did in an amazing way! I met Jerry Williamson, who truly became my "God Mother" in the truest sense. She guided me solidly in my relationship with Jesus in a new way, better than that of the thirteen-year-old me. She gave me my first amplified Bible, and I began reading, understanding, and loving it. Always before in my life, the Bible was difficult for me to understand. Up until then, I only had the little King James Bible I won at church reciting the twenty-third Psalm when I was six years old. I started reading Scripture and listening to God as I prayed, rather than talking the whole time. I could not get enough of the Bible, and the book of John, in particular, became one of my favorite books. I fell in love with this wonderful, loving, strong, and in-control God/man called Jesus.

Now I was experiencing the benefit of the "Son-light" I was meant to experience, and the Holy Spirit was joined with my Spirit in a new way also. I had come out of the kitchen of my heart into the "living room" where Jesus and the Holy Spirit of God dwell, and I was getting to know Jesus for real! Not long after that I discovered and created the image of the "Tree of Excellence" and began researching and using it as a life analogy. Then I discovered what God said about it, so I began using the analogy of the tree to life in my teaching alongside of Biblical teaching.

Rain, Rain, Go Away—Come Again Some Other Day!

If you live long enough, you will have a bit of rain mixed with the sunshine of life.

I married, gave birth to four beautiful children, have enjoyed great family times, and have had some wonderful performance, directing, teaching, and business experiences. All these represent warmth and sunshine to me.

There is also rain in life, which can cause great growth in many areas. It takes sunshine and rain, or water, to make a tree grow and be able to utilize the good nutrients available to it. Too much sun with no rain creates a desert. And too much rain with no sun also devastates.

Now it was time for the rain to come. I don't like standing out in the rain, even though I may need the water. Do you? There had been some stormy rain or problems in my life previously that scared me. But now I was planted in good soil, anchored, drinking in good reading material, and watching and listening to good positive information. I was soaking up good health habits as I took care of my body. And I had my spiritual electrical plug connected to the power source of God through Jesus and receiving full spectrum Spirit "Son-light" through His Word, the Bible. I did not realize it, but I was ready for the rainstorms to come.

Trees Have to Endure Storms to Be Strong, and so do we.

31

So much of who you are is shaped by the storms in your life. Fear of problems can turn into trust, such as memory lapses on stage, where in a fraction of a second trusting God puts escaped words back in your mind. Problems enrich you because they cause you to trust that there is an answer, and you feel great when the answer comes! My storms have caused me to rely on Jesus' strength and faithfulness to see my way safely through to the other side of the storm. Jesus' strength allows me to, not only wait out the storm with hope, but to **dance in the rain!**

> Jesus' strength allows you to,
> not only wait out the storm with hope,
> but to dance in the rain!

It reminds me of the eagle, who in a storm leaves the perceived safety of the nest, locks its wings and allows the "breath or wind of God" to carry it safely above the storm. Some pilots have been known to see eagles as high as fifteen to twenty thousand feet above the storm clouds. God has carried me above my storms and I know He will do the same for you.

My Storms

God helped me to recover from a performance memory phobia I developed while performing with the current Miss America of that time, when I forgot my lines on stage. I wanted the earth to open and swallow me right then and there. Can you relate? I had never had a memory slip before in all the many lines of dialogue on stage or in singing hundreds of lyrics to many songs. After that, I resolved never to sing again or do dramatic lines without a way to have words in front of me, somehow. The experience truly petrified me. I even wrote words on the face of my prop baby as I sang a beautiful lullaby song!

I will never forget the day on stage when I decided to trust Jesus and His Holy Spirit to prompt me with words if there was a memory problem. That was a scary thing for me, as up until then I had always figured a way to cleverly devise lyrics or lines in front of me for a memory crutch or prompt.

I was on the fashion show ramp stage above the huge audience of nearly two thousand people making my "solo flight" without my usual word crutch. I began the song, and all was going well. Then suddenly the old familiar panic, complete with seeing red behind my eyes, hit me. What were the next words? I had no idea! This all happened in a fraction of a second. I cried out to God in my mind, and in that same fraction of a second the music cue was there and so were the words! Now music is a brain memory hook and natural cue as discussed in chapter 6. But this was more than the natural musical cue kicking in. I was in a panic, which tends to shut down the brain's memory responses. It was an amazing experience, and I will always remember the incredible joy of having the Holy Spirit calm me and prompt me perfectly—all in a fraction of a second. After that, it became easier to trust every time I was in a scary or vulnerable place.

Jesus carried me through many family crises. I fought hard through prayer and listening for guidance from God's Word, the Bible, for a precious family member to keep the baby she was thinking of giving up for adoption. Jesus was amazing through that situation and answered my prayers in miraculous ways. He showed me He was trustworthy in every circumstance, even when I wanted to "deck" fellow Christian well-intenders who were giving me the cultural, politically correct advice to give the baby away. They were wrong! The baby stayed with our family, and Jesus has continued to answer prayers throughout that child's life.

I was jolted with the sudden death of a grand-baby who was one week from turning one year of age. Going through that heavy loss with our beautiful daughter and son-in-law was gut wrenching. But Jesus allowed me to audibly hear the baby's voice laughing after his death, and I knew he was with Jesus, that He was holding him, and that I would see him again. Jesus knew I needed to be reassured by hearing that precious baby laugh. I am inserting a letter from the father of that precious little child on what would have been his eighteenth birthday.

DECEMBER 8, 2013

Most people we meet don't know the story of Issac Christian, an incredible little boy who forever changed the journey of our lives.

My wife and I had been married for only a couple of years when our first son Isaac came into the world on December 8, 1995. As new parents, we were overjoyed (and overwhelmed) at this new little life that came into our world.

Our lives were instantly filled with hopes and dreams for him. He brought joy and laughter to our household, very much to his namesake, which means "He laughs" in Hebrew. Of course, as new parents, those hopes and dreams were tempered by the reality of having a newborn—the (lack of) sleep, the crying, and, of course, the diapers.

As the days went on, my wife and I continued to discover what it meant to "love someone beyond yourself." Becoming a parent helped me realize how awesome a responsibility it was and how much sacrifice all parents (including my own) make for their kids. There is absolutely nothing a parent would not do for their own child. It made sense to me now.

Fast forward to the week of Thanksgiving. It was our Monday night routine of reading a story, a prayer, and tucking him in to bed ready for the next day, and then off to bed. Little did we know our lives would forever be changed.

Tuesday, November 26, 1996. We woke up to the indescribable horror. Isaac was dead.

Isaac had passed away in the middle of the night due to SIDS (Sudden Infant Death Syndrome), something that still remains a mystery to medical science. The deep anguish we felt, the doubts, pain, hopelessness, and questioning was like an engulfing cloud around us, and it was painful to even breathe. We could not go on.

Why? What did we do to deserve this?

Honestly, we don't know why, but we do know that NOBODY deserves this. Kids generally outlive their parents, not the other way around. Did we do something to cause this? Did we put him to sleep wrong? We continually second-guessed ourselves. We did take some solace, what little we found, in the fact that the autopsy revealed that we did nothing wrong and the "mystery" of his death helped alleviate the blame that we could have easily put on ourselves. Still, however, the pain was deep, and despite people's best intention to comfort us, it would not bring him back.

Now, as we look back on this life-altering event many years ago, I cannot help but realize how much this chapter in our life has shaped our view of the world and our compassion for those who are hurting. We have come to realize and acknowledge something beyond ourselves that grounds us and keeps us steady despite what storms may come our way (oh, and little did we realize that there would be more of life's storms).

To say that we've "moved on" from this now, eighteen years later, having had subsequent children does not hide the fact that we still miss him and have not forgotten him. We remember this time in our lives with a deep sense of reflection and amazement to the power of faith to hold us steady when all of life is unsteady.

We have all heard the saying, "When life gives you lemons, make lemonade." Well, making lemonade out of lemons seems like a nice little thing to say when someone is hurting, but it really isn't true. For us, it's more like learning to swim in an ocean of lemon juice. It hurts. It stings. It takes work—hard work. However, when you do learn to "swim in it," you focus less on the pool and more on making the constant progress towards your destination.

Happy 18th birthday Isaac Christian Domingo.
Mom and I love you.

All through these gut-wrenching life losses and experiences, surgeries and unknown futures, God has been there to hold and heal. I have had numerous times of thinking I would lose my mind because of difficult family relationships. Betrayal in life, be it family or friends, is never an easy thing to deal with. But by choosing to love and forgive those who have hurt me deeply, I have a peace that only comes from God. Besides, not forgiving would be like drinking poison, expecting the person who hurt me to die. With Jesus' help I have stayed committed to my precious husband and marriage vows, and I deeply love all my children, their spouses, and all my grandchildren. As a result, there have been no divorces, and I didn't "kill" any of my children in their teens! Can you relate?

When I was in my early fifties, God gave me a "heads-up" in my Spirit, as I listened to our women's ministry leader at the time share the agonizing experience of caring for and losing her mother little by little to Alzheimer's disease.

And then for more than sixteen years or so, I found myself caring for my aging parents, Mother with Alzheimer's disease, and Daddy in his struggles with Mom's disease. I flew fifteen hundred miles every three months, then every month, and then every two weeks to my family home for the first three years. Then I cared for them for five years in our home as their full-time caregiver, until my health declined severely from the stress. Then for the next eight years or so I oversaw their care in care facilities until they passed.

Mom passed while I was away on a trip, but God, in His love and great care, provided my lovely daughters to be with her, my younger daughter staying all night. God took care of details for me, like my need to have a familial loving person and spirit with her, as Mother didn't consciously know us anymore. I had always wanted to be with her at her passing, and be that loving presence with her that understood her and her needs. My younger daughter was that, climbing in bed and stroking her gently and speaking and singing words of comfort. When I asked my daughter what she sang to Momma, she said she didn't know what to sing. But after asking for God's divine help, He put "Softly and Tenderly" in her heart and she sang the beautiful old hymn to Momma. What was so amazing about this was I could not let go of that song all day as she was passing, and I didn't know if my daughter knew the song. God even took care of the details of my desire to be in bed with Momma and to sing to her the song I used to sing to her all the time. I am so thankful for His provision. I knew Mom was physically loved on her way to be with Jesus.

God provided me the opportunity to share the experience of my dad accepting Christ, and to be with Daddy and hold his hand as he passed within a few days of his genuine union with Christ.

The experience of caring for my dear parents has brought many different kinds of joys and storms in my life, most of which I never could have foreseen. But Jesus knew all along, and He has tenderly held me, provided for me, and carried me through it all, just as the "Footprints in the Sand" poem indicates.

"*The times when you have seen only one set of footprints, is when I carried you.*"

Jesus has walked with me through all of my storms. He has given me miracle after miracle and allowed many challenging circumstances, but He has also given me compassion, strength, courage, wisdom, understanding, and joy in every storm. He has, in fact, carried me over the storms to safety. He has done that for me, and He is a huge God who will do that for you as you trust Him.

Your life gives you so much richness to share as a speaker and singer. "Just Look for the Silver Lining," as the old song says. The storms can become the source from which your strength and best messages of authenticity come from. Just as a tree must be put out in the garden to "harden off" (which means get used to the rain, wind, and colder temperatures to become strong), you must also know that in the storm you will only become stronger with Jesus in you and at your back holding you.

Remember, trees get attacked when they're weak. The root of bitterness can open you up to destruction. The roots of a tree are sometimes attacked first. Then bad bugs sense a problem and go after new growth and destroy leaves and the tree's ability to transform nutrients to fruit through photosynthesis. Your body and mind roots (relationship with yourself), tree-top branches and leaves (your relationships with others), and your crop of relational fruit are all at risk. Be on the lookout for roots of bitterness, bad attitudes, anger, jealousy, all sorts of immorality, hostility, worship of anything other than God Himself, selfishness, selfish ambition, dealings with spirits other than the Holy Spirit of God, lust, impurity, quarreling, drunkenness, complaining, speaking ill of others, not caring for your physical health and nutrition, sleep, water intake, etc. These will destroy your tree health, as these are the bad bugs that "take you out."

So, be careful and choose to find your safety in Jesus and His advice during those stormy times in life, using His fruit of love, joy, peace, patience, kindness, goodness, faithfulness, gentleness, and self-control, coupled with Colossians clothes of tender-hearted mercy, compassion, humility, forgiveness, understanding, and love over all. If you live by the Spirit, your "Tree of Excellence" will remain healthy and strong, and you will be a blessing to others with your awesome fruit and your messages as a speaker. The amazing thing about trees is that healthy trees are not attacked even when in close proximity to a weak tree ravaged by bad bugs. Bad bugs can go after a weak tree and not even consider attacking the healthy tree very close to it. This is good news for you and your speaking messages. You can thrive even when others around you are faltering. Jesus has your back!

Why am I telling you this, and what does this have to do with voice? You are like the "Tree of Excellence," strong in the storm, and like a diamond. All the storms are like the cuts in a diamond. A diamond only becomes beautiful when it is cut and polished and sparkles in the light. You are more beautiful and stronger with the cuts of life that God allows, which make you resilient and brilliant in His light. Your voice becomes more impactful as you stand strong and shine forth your experiences in life to bless others.

Read on to get a better understanding of who you are, who Jesus really is, and as you do, you will begin to connect the dots. You and your credibility as a speaker depend on your understanding that Jesus is real and that He has your best interest at heart. You must know the importance of yourself as the "Tree of Excellence," how you grow, thrive, and survive the storms, which only make you stronger and give you awesome opportunities to bless others. Understanding and application of these things will help you open to all Jesus has for you as a speaker. Your confidence as a speaker or singer is wrapped up in these truths.

Chapter 5

THE KEY THAT UNLOCKS GREATNESS IN YOU

"Not by might, nor by power, but by my Spirit, says the Lord Almighty—you will succeed because of my Spirit, though you are few and weak."
—Zechariah 4:6, (TLB)

Vocal Application: *Since your spirit guides your thoughts in your mind, which guides and influences your brain, which influences your body, you must allow God's Spirit to connect to and influence and guide your spirit, thereby enabling you to choose your thoughts well and experience complete health. The choices you make in how you think determine your confidence in speaking and*

*singing. How you think and communicate with
others when you speak or sing is dependent on
inspiration from your spirit, heart, mind and passions. God's Spirit is sound and will always give
you what you need when you need it. Your credibility as a speaker or singer is vital, and it depends
on this connection to God's Spirit and knowing
how to truly serve others with what they desire
from you. His Spirit in you truly unlocks your
significant greatness, and shines your spirit light
brightly to others in many ways.*

To begin connecting the dots you must understand that you are a triune person: spirit, mind, and body.

> *"Not by might, nor by power, but by my Spirit, says
> the Lord Almighty—you will succeed because of my
> Spirit, though you are few and weak."* —Zechariah
> 4:6, (TLB)

What a promise! It was given to the prophet, Zechariah, by the angel of the Lord, for King Zerubbabel, but it applies to you and me as well.

The book of Zechariah is a picture book that paints clear images or word pictures. Images are very important as you speak or sing because people are engaged with you as you paint clear pictures with your words from your authentic heart and self. **Also, the power in a picture is that you act or do on the outside what you picture or see on the inside.** As you give or paint great word pictures, you invoke great actions in others. Jesus spoke in great word pictures called parables, and He is a great example to us of the power in word pictures.

God is so faithful to be sure you see and hear what you need, when you need it, whether you are a prophet or not. So, the clear message of Zechariah is that you cannot muster enough might or power to succeed on your own. You need the Spirit of God to accomplish success of any kind, including your singing and speaking well.

> *"I will give you a new heart and put a new Spirit in you; I will remove from you your heart of stone and give you a heart of flesh."* —Ezekiel 36:26, (NIV)

> *"So there is now no condemnation awaiting those who belong to Christ Jesus. For the power of the life-giving Spirit—and this power is [yours] through Christ Jesus—has freed [you] from the vicious circle of sin and death."* —Romans 8:1, (TLB)

> *"Therefore, if anyone is in Christ he is a new creation. The old has gone, the new is here!"* —2 Corinthians 5:17, (NIV)

Note that I use spirit, mind, body, when referring to you as a triune person. In society the order of your human trinity usually is stated: body, mind, and spirit. But in the Biblical book of First Thessalonians it clearly gives you God's view of this order, which is referred to in this way in all of Scripture.

> *"May the God of peace himself make you entirely*
> *pure and devoted to God; and may your spirit and*
> *soul [mind,] and body be kept strong and blameless*
> *until that day when the Lord Jesus Christ comes*
> *back again."* — 1Thessalonians 5:23, (TLB)

This is the order I will use to honor the Spirit of God and the strength and power that comes from His Spirit to you. You are a spirit person who happens to live in a body with a brain and mind. Because modern science (according to Dr. Caroline Leaf)[1,2] has proven that the spirit drives the mind; the mind drives the brain; and the brain drives the body, it is appropriate that the order is spirit, mind/brain, body as well.

The top of the tree is representative of your spirit and your relationship with God and others. You are a child of God. It is made up of branches and leaves. You now know that the roots are taking in water and nutrients to feed your tree through your body and mind. But how do you keep your leaves green in season and out, and produce fruit that is meaningful?

As stated previously, the nutrients are pulled up to the leaves through the trunk, or core of your tree where Jesus lives and permeates, to the branches. Now there is a miraculous thing that happens. Through the miracle of photosynthesis, the water and nutrients are taken into the leaves and are transformed by the power of full spectrum sunlight into life-giving energy that produces life-giving leaves that produce blossoms and fruit.

I want you to think of that special full spectrum sunlight as Spirit light from God's Son, Jesus. It is "Son-light" and has great power to transform all your relationships with the fruit of the Spirit, which are love, joy, peace, patience, kindness, goodness, faithfulness, gentleness, and self-control. By having your spirit plugged into the power source of Jesus, the Holy Spirit can truly empower you to grow and feed others with this amazing fruit that comes from His Spirit.

As mentioned before, when people speak of the "law of attraction" they are simply stating the truth that there is power in operation in the fruit of God's Spirit. Love, joy, peace, patience, kindness, goodness, faithfulness, gentleness, and self-control—when exhibited—will always attract others and good to you. When you operate in the fruit of the Spirit, your energy will always resonate high, as that is the way God designed you to resonate and become the "light of the world."

> *"This is the message we have heard from him and declare to you: God is light; in him there is no darkness at all. If we claim to have fellowship with him and yet walk in the darkness, we lie and do not live out the truth. But if we walk in the light, as he is in the light, we have fellowship with one another, and the blood of Jesus, his son, purifies us from all sin."*—1 John 1:5–7, (NIV)

> *"The sun will no more be your light by day, nor will the brightness of the moon shine on you, for the Lord will be your everlasting light, and your God will be your glory."*—Isaiah 60:19, (NIV)

But just as the Holy Spirit of God produces the best life-giving light and good fruit in us, there is a converse result of a spirit not connected to God and His power. **The list of "bad" fruit is compelling and important to a speaker or singer because spirit of intent and lack of credibility show no matter how you try to hide them or fool your audience.**

"But when you follow your own wrong inclinations your life will produce these evil results: impure thoughts, eagerness for lustful pleasure, idolatry, spiritism (that is encouraging the activity of demons), hatred and fighting, jealousy and anger, constant effort to get the best for yourself, complaints and criticisms, the feeling that everyone else is wrong except those in your own little group—and there will be wrong doctrine, envy, murder, drunkenness, wild parties, and all that sort of thing. Let me tell you again, as I have before, that anyone living that sort of life will not inherit the Kingdom of God."—Galatians 5:19–21, (TLB)

Look at the image of the tree top again. The branches represent different areas of life and relationships of your life. As stated in chapter 3, one area would be your financial branches of being a business owner or employee. Who are the people who need your good "fruit" exhibited there? Make a list of them.

Women 50-65

Church Groups

Senior Centers

Hospice

Another set of branches represent your community and volunteering, such as church and civic organizations, friendships, etc. Who needs to have your special, unique, and loving fruit exhibited there? Make a list of these people.

NBP

Elaine

Refugee

And finally, a great group of branches represent your family. You are a child of God, and your parents, a sister or brother to siblings, a spouse, an aunt or uncle to nieces and nephews, a mother or father to children, a grandmother or grandfather to grandchildren, etc. These folks, I guarantee, need your God-supplied fruit given to them. I will talk about balance with you in chapter 14, but suffice it to say, the picture of you as the "Tree of Excellence" will help you keep track of your relationships and fruit. It becomes a great tool for being able to see at a glance how you are doing in your different relationship branch categories. You must be a fruit inspector and cultivator of your own fruit. Make a list of family members who need a dose of good fruit today.

Peter, Andrew, Alex, Adam, Mom, Sharon
Tim, Patrick, Matthew, Andrews., David
David's boys', A & K's kids, Michael
Tara

Remember, God has called you to "bear much fruit," and "apart from Him, you can do nothing."

> *"You have not chosen Me, but I have chosen you and I have appointed and placed and purposefully planted you, so that you would go and bear fruit and keep on bearing, and that your fruit will remain and be lasting, so that whatever you ask of the Father in My name [as My representative] He may give to you."* —John 15:16, (AMP)

> *"I am the vine; you are the branches. If you remain in me and I in you, you will bear much fruit; apart from me you can do nothing."* —John 15:5, (NIV)

We are told in Scripture to renew our minds daily.

> *"I plead with you to give your bodies to God. Let them be a living sacrifice, holy, the kind he can*

accept. When you think of what he has done for you, is this too much to ask? Don't copy the behavior and customs of this world, but be a new [transformed] and different person with a fresh newness in all you do and think." —Romans 12:1–2, (TLB)

"And do not be conformed to this world; but be transformed by the renewing of your mind, that you may prove what is that good and acceptable and perfect will of God" —Romans 12:2, (NKJV)

As you renew your mind daily with the power of God's Word, and agree with its truth, you are equipped to deal with others lovingly, joyfully, peacefully, patiently, kindly, and gently in a faithful, good, generous, and self-controlled way. And you take better care of yourself in the root areas of mind and body care.

God knows everything about you, and His Word has the power to heal you and help you live this life to your best and fulfill your purpose here on planet earth. (See chapter 13 for more on God's purpose in you.)

In order to be more successful in all you do, you will need to consider protection for your roots and your fruit. You have access to the full armor of God as protection from anything or anyone who tries to come against you. As a speaker, you feel vulnerable and in need of covering or protection at times. I know I do. It is a joy to know I feel safe,

PRAYER

SALVATION

SPIRIT

BIBLE

GOD'S APPROVAL

FAITH

TRUTH

PEACE

so I remind myself daily of God's armor and choose to consciously put it on. His armor is where I am strong with His strength, and protected from evil.

> *"I want to remind you that your strength must come from the Lord's mighty power within you. Put on all of God's armor so that you will be able to stand safe against all strategies and tricks of Satan. For we are not fighting against people made of flesh and blood, but against persons without bodies—the evil rulers of the unseen world, those mighty satanic beings and great evil princes of darkness that rule this world; and against huge numbers of wicked spirits in the spirit world. So use every piece of God's armor to resist the devil whenever he attacks, and when it is all over, you will still be standing up. But to do this, you will need the strong belt of truth and the breastplate of God's approval. Wear shoes that are able to speed you on as you preach the Good News of peace with God. In every battle, you will need faith as your shield to stop the fiery darts aimed at you by Satan. And you will need the helmet of salvation and the sword of the Spirit—which is the Word of God. Pray all the time. Ask God for anything in line with the Holy Spirit's wishes. Plead with him, reminding him of your needs, and keep praying earnestly for all Christians everywhere."*—Ephesians 6:10–18, (TLB)

Paul's advice in this whole portion of Scripture is all about using God's Word, as your spiritual protection and strength. The image of the armor is a great picture. The belt of truth, the Bible, goes on to secure the breastplate of God's approval. How do we know what He approves of if we aren't familiar with and using His Word in our lives to secure our heart protector, the breastplate of living rightly?

Then there are the shoes of peace. You must put these on and be ready to run with them, being sure you always leave tracks of the peace of God. His peace keeps you steady and sure footed.

In every battle faith is your shield and protects you from all fiery arrows aimed at you. I love this picture because it is of a huge shield, as big as a door, with wet leather wrapped around it so that even fire is put out when it comes in contact with it. Faith is huge and overpowers any fear or negative fiery attitudes or situations that try to come against you. What a cool shield!

And you will need the helmet of salvation. Why a helmet? Your brain is housed by that helmet, the vessel of your spirit, thoughts, and body control. God's Word is a helmet of protection to your whole being.

All the armor thus far is **defensive**. But the sword of the Spirit, which is the Word of God, is very different. It is **offensive** and a sure weapon against any and all evil or obstacles in your life. While the Word of God is seen in the armor as many defensive tools covering you and equipping you well, the use of the Word of God, as a sword, takes on the offensive power to destroy falsehoods and anything trying to come against you. When you watch a football game, you are thrilled when the offense makes a touchdown. You are also happy when the defense stops the other team from scoring. The

Bible, as seen in the full armor, is your best **defense** and **offense** for winning the game of life and speech!

> *"For the word of God is living and powerful, and sharper than any two-edged sword, piercing even to the division of soul and spirit, and of joints and marrow, and is a discerner of the thoughts and intents of the heart."* —Hebrews 4:12, (NKJV)

Then finally prayer is the plume on top of the helmet shaped like praying hands. Prayer is both **defensive** and **offensive**. It is a protection and a sound weapon against evil, and very effective. Use your God-given armor. It works. A speaker or singer needs a full set to be effective with a sound message full of truth and enthusiasm delivered through an authentic heart and spirit.

> *"The Spirit gives life; the flesh counts for nothing. The words I have spoken to you—they are full of the Spirit and life."* —John 6:63 (NIV)

Chapter 6

WHAT YOU THINK
DOES MATTER!

*"For God hath not given us the spirit of fear; but
of power, and of love, and of a sound mind."*
                                    —2 Timothy 1:7, (KJV)

Vocal application: *You were created with love for
love, power, and success with a sound mind and
ability to reach any potential you choose. The balance of open controlled voice, spirit, mind (soul),
and body help you discover the "sweet spot" of
your voice. God did not put fear in your DNA. Fear
is learned and can be unlearned as well, enabling
you to speak and sing with joy, confidence, and
purpose. Choice of thoughts and actions is critical
to your success and overall health. Choose wisely
by knowing what your mind is chattering to you.
You can choose to be anything you desire. It is up*

to you by choosing to use your sound mind. God's Word cuts through all your "stuff" and exposes your inner thoughts and desires (Hebrews 4:12). Pay attention to that amazing guidance.

Why is how you think so important? You are a learner and a teacher in life, and there is great responsibility associated there. Your thinking is critical to your speaking and singing because it reflects your relationship with yourself and God.

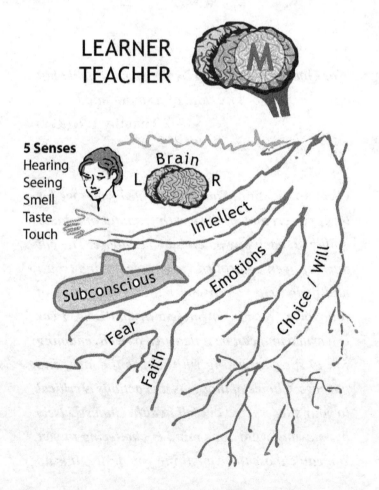

LEARNER TEACHER

5 Senses
Hearing
Seeing
Smell
Taste
Touch

Brain
L   R

Intellect

Subconscious

Emotions

Choice / Will

Fear

Faith

Vocal and presentation success both depend on you understanding how you think and why—one of the keys to finding your vocal "sweet spot." What you read, listen to, and watch, as well as who you choose to "hang out" with, influence your mind "roots," thus your attitudes and beliefs. It is important to protect your root systems with healthy positive influencers. Just as it is important to take good care of the body "roots" of your tree (chapter 7), it is equally important to master the care of the "roots" of your mind. Choice is the key here. You have a choice to choose life, good, and blessing, or not!

> *"This day I call the heavens and the earth as witnesses against you that I have set before you life and death, blessings and curses. Now choose life, so that you and your children may live."* —Deuteronomy 30:19, (NIV)

> *"So letting your sinful nature control your mind leads to death. But letting the Spirit [of God] control your mind leads to life and peace."* —Romans 8:6, (NLT)

Have you ever felt so stressed you wanted to run away or put your head in the sand like an ostrich attempting to make the world go away—like on stage and scared to death? I have. But I have also experienced great happiness, love, and elation—like presenting at my absolute best, and how good that feels. There is a vast difference in the two as to how you and I feel all over, physically, mentally, spiritually, and, certainly, emotionally.

How do you feel physically and emotionally when you are stressed and want to run away? How do you feel physically and emotionally when you are experiencing love and happiness or elation and success? How and what you think in any situation influences your emotions, attitudes, and body responses, thus your health, happiness, and, ultimately, your behavior and voice.

I want you to experience on a regular basis the good thoughts and emotions of love, joy, success, and health. There is great good waiting for you in understanding and putting into practice healthy thinking.

What Lies Behind the Windows of Your Mind?

According to Dr. Caroline Leaf, neuroscience researcher, the brain and thoughts lie behind the windows of your mind. She states that science and research agree that:

- The body mind connection is real and is a critical key to physical, mental, and emotional wellness.
- How and what you think are keys to successful, happy, stress-free living.
- Thoughts create electrical-chemical reactions from the brain to the body.
- Thoughts are intimately linked to emotions and affect your attitudes, body, and behaviors.
- Eighty-seven percent of all illnesses can be attributed to thought life.
- Only thirteen percent of all illnesses can be attributed to diet, genetics, and the environment.

Western culture creates toxic thinking, producing toxic emotions that are linked to chronic diseases such as migraines, hypertension, strokes, cancer, skin problems, diabetes, infections, and allergies, to name a few.

Science and research also agree that you can think yourself clever, calm, healthy, and successful; you can think yourself into forgiving and forgiveness, out of worry and anxiety, out of bitterness and resentment; and you can think yourself in control of your emotions and out of stress![1]

Choose life and blessing, just as Deuteronomy told you. You were created by love for love and life, not fear and destruction. You learn fear. Love is your default, so choosing to think yourself healthy and successful is a powerfully loving thing to do.

We know that the Holy Spirit infuses your spirit, which influences your mind, which in turn controls brain chemistry, and brain chemistry controls your body chemistry. In Dr. Caroline Leaf's book *Switch On Your Brain, the Key to Peak Happiness, Thinking and Health,* published in 2013 by Baker Books. *Think & Eat Yourself Smart*, published in 2016 by Baker Publishing Group, she states you can change your brain wiring with hope and excitement for the future. That brings my mind to this scripture:

> *"For I know the plans I have for you,"* declares the
> LORD, *"plans to prosper you and not to harm you,*
> *plans to give you hope and a future."*—Jeremiah
> 29:11, (NIV)

When you know God has your back, it is fun to think about the future. More on your future in the chapter on Purpose.

Your mind consists of the nonconscious, or subconscious, and the conscious. Both deal with thoughts. The nonconscious runs ninety to ninety-nine percent of your thinking and thought building. It can perform four hundred billion actions per second, operates twenty-four hours a day, and drives the conscious cognitive level of your mind. The conscious mind performs only about two thousand actions per second. It is where up to ten percent of the mind action takes place and is much slower than the nonconscious. All the consciousness you experience boils down to roughly a mere fifty-eight minutes out of each day. The nonconscious, or subconscious, basically runs your behavior.[2]

Information comes in through the five senses (sight, smell, hearing, taste, and touch) in the conscious mind. You also express yourself and experience the world through these senses. Then the information passes to the subconscious, or nonconscious mind, where you begin to take it captive and begin the process of thinking and choosing. It now is a physical thought with genetic expression. This physical thought also impacts your conscious thinking and behavior and what you say or do with the thought.[2]

Every thought is electrically and chemically attached to an emotion. No thought is void of an emotion attached to it. They are inseparable. The progression is like this:

- Thoughts attach to and stimulate emotions.
- Emotions result in attitudes.
- Attitudes produce behavior and bodily reactions (like vocal stress).

When on stage you must become aware of your thoughts because the electrical chemical energy that emits from you by way of your thoughts affects your audience and reflects back to you. When you choose to openly think love, blessing, and good as you give your gift to your audience, they are strengthened and reflect positive good back to you. But when you are thinking about you and your self-concern, such as "what if they don't like me or my gift," you are sending out negative brain energy, and they get nervous for you and reflect back the same negative energy.

Your thoughts either build confidence or erode it. It is your choice. In 1971, Albert Mehrabian published his research on the seven percent rule. He concluded that credibility is assigned to fifty-five percent body language, thirty-eight percent to voice and vocal variation, and only seven percent to the words spoken. All of that is controlled by your thought process.

An exercise I do in my workshops is to do a kinesiology test on a volunteer to make sure they are a good test case. The brain knows your name and who you are, or not. If the person says their name, they will be strong physically. If they say they are a name that is not their real name, the body becomes weak.

Then I blindfold the person, and without a word from anyone, I have the audience (by way of a picture being held up for them to see) think very genuine, loving thoughts and direct those thoughts to the volunteer. They grow strong. Next I have the audience send the second kind of very negative, toxic brain energy to the volunteer, and they grow weak in physical strength. Then I have them send what the volunteer thinks is a third energy, which is really love and positive thoughts again. The volunteer becomes strong again. When I take the blindfold off, and all can see what different energies of thought were sent and the responses of the volunteer, it proves the point that what you think definitely affects those around you. You, as a speaker, send out your loving, authentic gift-giving energy to your audience, and they respond well, and lean in and want more of you.

Negative destructive thinking is electrochemically attached to destructive emotions, producing negative destructive attitudes and behaviors, creating destructive electrochemical reactions in the body. As a result, you don't feel well, and are set up to become very ill, or "bomb" on stage.

In the same way, positive, rejuvenated, and hopeful thinking produces good attitudes, physical feelings, and behaviors. Depending on the quality of the thought and emotion you choose to entertain, you can be helped or harmed by their corresponding chemicals to your brain and body. According to Dr. Candace Pert, a pioneering neuroscientist, emotions and their biological components establish the crucial link between the mind and the body. She calls these bio-chemicals "molecules of emotions." These molecules of emotions create copies of your thought life and corresponding emotions, and carry the information to your whole body potentially changing cellular structure on the outside and even DNA on the inside.[1]

Both Sides Now

The old song—"Both Sides Now" (1969, Reprise Records, sung by Joni Mitchell—) is true of the brain. The brain has distinct left and right hemispheres. Make two fists and hold them side by side with thumbs on top. This represents the two hemispheres of your brain in similar shape and size. Men's brains are usually larger than women's, but female brains are more compact.

We used to think you only used each side exclusively and separately for different functions. The left hemisphere was once thought to be responsible **only** for linear, logical, and analytic functions. The right hemisphere was thought to be **only** your creative, artsy side where rhythm and color lived.

The truth is, the brain has mirror neurons in both sides, and the two sides must work together rather than in separate functions. You must use both sides together, the left side seeing details, then the big picture, while the right side sees the big picture, then the details.[1]

Do You Like Puzzles?

A puzzle is a great representation of how the two hemispheres of the brain must work together to be healthy. The puzzle pieces are the necessary details of the overall big picture. The left side of your brain sees the details, or pieces first, and how they fit into and create a big picture. The right side of your brain sees the big picture first and then the details, or perceives there are detailed pieces to be fitted into the big picture.

Math could seem too difficult if you were not taught to think with both sides of your brain at once. With the equation, 2x2=4, two times two equals four. The left side of your brain first sees the details of two groups of two, and that it is equal to four, the big picture. The right side of your brain sees four as the big picture first, but also must see how the details of two groups of two make up the big picture, four. Understanding comes with both sides of the brain working in harmony with the details and the big picture.[1]

All areas of your life must be congruent with the functions of both sides of the brain working in mirror images to be healthy and efficient. Your brain also produces mirror—or double memories—in both hemispheres. Your brain was designed with both sides working in synergy, so the more you think, the more you understand and remember. That is great news for those of us who speak or sing and are needing to memorize lyrics and content.

There is so much more to this subject, and I am only scratching the surface for you to help you understand the importance of healthy thinking for vocal success and success in all of life. Three great books by Dr. Caroline Leaf for better understanding would be: *Who Switched Off my Brain: Controlling Toxic Thoughts and Emotions*, published in 2009 by Thomas Nelson; 2. *Switch On Your Brain: The Key to Peak Happiness, Thinking and Health,* published in 2013 by Baker Books; 3. *Think & Eat Yourself Smart,* published in 2016 by Baker Publishing Group.

Where Did I Put My Keys? Where Did My Words Go?

Memory is a great and complicated thing. It serves you well, and sometimes seems to get lost, often in moments of stress or when speaking and singing. But because of the double mirror memories, when calm returns, usually your memory returns as well.

Memorizing and deep thought make your brain stronger. As a result, you are happier and healthier as well. Speaking and singing require you to think deeply and concentrate. Our multitasking culture takes you away from healthy deep thought. Speaking and singing use deep thought and memory, and are healthy and definitely good for you. And yes, you can memorize well with a little discipline by using your amazing thinking skills.

Memory is stored long-term in the neuron cells. These cells are called dendrites, and they grow, strengthen, and pass information along to other cells. They connect with other cells by way of synapses, electrochemically jumping from one cell to the other and creating more connections and feedback loops to your body. Remember, your brain performs about four hundred billion actions each second, and you are only conscious of about two thousand.

Spread your fingers out as you hold your arm up.

This looks like a tree of sorts, with your arm being the trunk, called an axon, and your fingers being the dendrites, or branches of memory. You have one hundred trillion dendrites in your brain, and each one can produce or grow seventy thousand branches. This means you have about three million years of information capacity in your brain.[1]

Your memory becomes strong by multisensory input (sight, smell, taste, touch, and hearing), review of information within twenty-four hours, and again in seven days and ongoing. This strengthens your memory neuron cells by wrapping the axon trunks with myelin, like a sheath to reinforce them. The brain cleans house at night and destroys cells that are not stable or strong. Have you ever lost information overnight and wondered why? Brain cleanup happened, and your information was not reinforced enough. So, last-minute cramming for a speech or class is not very effective, because it is difficult to really reinforce your thoughts adequately.

The more senses you engage, the stronger your memory becomes, because your brain makes multisensory associations well. Painting word pictures with your message, using as many senses as possible, helps you remember your speech or song, and helps your audience remember your message and you. If you see, hear, smell, taste, and feel your message, you will experience it and remember it better. You can strengthen the memory if you create what is called a "Mind Map" of the speech or song. My husband and I have the privilege of knowing Mr. Tony Buzan, who developed mind mapping. A mind map is simply a map of the talk laid out with a central theme and branches of thought extending from the central theme. Use of key words in capital letters, color, and pictures help your brain grab and hold on to the information. I rarely use notes when I have made a mind map of my workshop or talk, because after creating the mind map, my brain literally sees it in color and order. In fact, the tree in this book is a kind of mind map (see chapter 3).

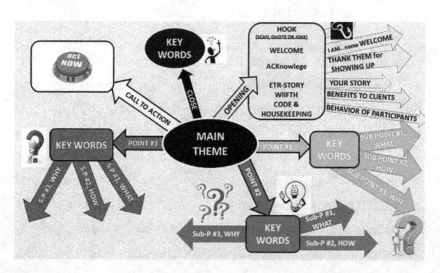

Mind maps are very helpful for anyone who wants to take notes or create a talk or speech. Your mind quickly grabs and memorizes the core topic in the center with the branching of ideas using color, pictures, and simple key words in capital letters to trigger your thoughts. My clients learn to love mind maps in creating their message talks because mind mapping is so effective.

Mind maps allow you to memorize and deliver your message from an authentic heart versus trying to memorize words, or as in reading your typed message. You have your main and sub ideas in front of you, and you know what you want to say as your mind map triggers your thoughts by all the associative branches you have created. This is memorizing without the rote sort of memorization. You still, of course, rehearse your topic and thoughts, but mind mapping allows you to remain present and authentic in delivery.

Using outrageous pictures associated with known things or places also helps the memory. For instance, when choosing to create a memory of the Biblical book of Philippians, chapter four, verse eight, I built a sequenced stack of pictures to help my brain remember the list of things to think about from that scripture.

My known thing or place was my body. *"Whatever things are true and noble,"* I see a huge Bible on top of the head of my imaginary genie-like man (sort of a Mr. Clean), and a big **N** burned into his forehead. Then, *"whatever things are right and pure,"* I see him flexing his huge right arm muscles and carrying a bottle of Purex in his strong bent left arm. Then, *"whatever things are lovely,"* I see a fancy valentine heart lit up flashing in his chest. *"Whatever things are admirable* in others," I see a gold belt made of AAA's around his waist. *"Whatever is of excellence,"* I laugh to see a fig leaf in its appropriate place on the body. Then lastly in the list is to think of *"whatever is praise worthy,"* and I see his knees bent backward toward heaven praising God. It is a crazy outrageous stack, but from its first creation I have never forgotten it!

If you use colorful, multisensory and emotional images in memorizing material to speak or sing, you will remember the material better. When you have any information you want to remember, review it within twenty-four hours and again within seven days and beyond, and you will be amazed at how easy it is to remember long into the future.

I bet you can remember certain songs from your past rather well. This is because music connects both sides of the brain efficiently and is easily reinforced by hearing and singing the words repetitively over time. Music serves as a memory "hook," just as color and pictures do with words. I was asked to sing for a wedding recently with short notice. To my happy amazement, I remembered the words to one of the songs that I hadn't sung for twenty years or more. They came flooding to me on first rehearsal. That is the power of your God-given wonderful mind and memory when you choose to use it.

Choose Your Path!

There is good news to all this information. You can choose how you think, thus your health, well-being, and positive successful behavior patterns. You can **choose** to speak, sing, and present your message well by choosing what and how to think. Then by developing the message, memory, and delivery skills, determining to implement them, you experience the joy of a successful presentation. These skills are my gift to you in this book, and they develop and are enhanced by working with me in one of my coaching programs.

*"We demolish arguments and every pretention that
sets itself up against the knowledge of God, and we
take captive every thought to make it obedient to
Christ."* —2 Corinthians 10:5, (NIV)

*"Do not conform to the pattern of this world, but **be
transformed by the renewing of your mind.** Then
you will be able to test and approve what God's will
is—his good, pleasing and perfect will."* —Romans
12:2, (NIV)

You Can Take Captive, Control, and Renew Your Thoughts

This is how it works. As stated before, the thoughts come in
through your five senses: sight, hearing, taste, touch/feel, and smell.
All but smell goes to the inner brain limbic system, to the thalamus or relay station. Smell bypasses the normal path of the thalamus and subsequent pathways and goes straight into the emotional
storage center, the amygdala, which is why strong emotional memories occur with certain smells.

The electrical thought then gathers chemicals and goes on to
the dendrites of memory in the cortex of the brain, where it looks
for familiar information and memories. Dr. Caroline Leaf calls this
a "breeze through the dendrite trees."[1]

Your First Attitude Check Point

This is your first chance to pay attention and decide to allow
a thought to help or harm you. When the memory is found in the

cortex, whether negative or positive, the brain sends the emotional thought to pick up more emotional chemicals. The question to yourself is, where have I seen or heard this before? When you are learning a song or speech message, you will come across old familiar stories to yourself, some empowering and some fearful and disempowering. Pay attention to what is going on in your thoughts.

You Get A Second Chance. Change Your Attitude and Control Your Emotional Thoughts

Now the electrochemical thought gets dropped into the emotional library called the amygdala. The emotions stored here are strong and reactive. They can override any reasoning power you have, so your power of choice to analyze and choose healthy thinking is critical at this stage.

You will always have a "gut" reaction from the emotions of the amygdala. Listen to your body so you can choose to analyze the thoughts that are creating those emotions. The good news is that the frontal cortex of reason is directly linked at this point, so you can choose to put a love/faith spin on any thought. If your thought is negative, you can rewrite the emotional response by **choosing** a thought that is positive, based on real truth or Bible based, which allows you to release the negative thought and emotion.

"…we take captive every thought to make it obedient to Christ Jesus." —2 Corinthians 10:5, (NIV)

This excerpt from the Bible is a powerful truth that will always serve you well in controlling your thoughts. You must pay attention to your physical state and check in with your thoughts, so you can take those thoughts captive and choose to dismiss negative thoughts and agree with positive truth and dwell on the positive. You will feel your physiology change from negative gut response to relaxed body response when you choose positivity and hope.

Consider if you were somewhere and asked to speak impromptu. The thought, "I am not prepared," breezes through your brain cortex and lands on a memory of when someone told you that you are not a good singer or speaker, or a memory of "bombing" a speech (first check point or attention). Now the thought gathers more chemicals, drops into the amygdala, and you have a gut reaction of stress and fear. Your stomach hurts, your heart pumps faster, etc. (second chance to take control).

You have a choice to agree with the bad memory or choose a new thought by saying out loud, "Stop! Thank you, brain, for sharing, but I am a great speaker or singer. I have a great repertoire of things to sing or speak on, and I can do this because Jesus loves me, gave me ability, and has my back."

You now have stopped the negative story and literally rewritten the experience, emotions, and reactions. And you feel your body relax and begin to gather fun excitement at the thought of doing the impromptu speech.

Turn Negative Thoughts into Hot Air, Your Third Chance to Take Emotional Electrochemical Thoughts Captive

The emotional electrochemical thought goes from your emotional library to the short-term memory, and activates the "thinker," or the C-shaped corpus callosum, which is the connective tissue that connects left and right brain hemispheres and responses. It allows you to access your reasoning skills to a greater level. With the benefit of the thinker in action, you **ask, answer**, and **discuss** the whole situation with yourself, using both sides of your brain. You can now choose to allow the emotional thought, if negative, to dissipate into hot air and not affect you negatively any longer (like the new thought of doing your impromptu talk). If you choose to hang on to the thought, it returns to the dendrites of memory and reinforces the negative or positive memory. The negative ones become black, dense, thorny memory dendrites and continue to pump negative destructive chemicals to your body, while the positive ones become healthy dense memories that promote healthy responses all over the brain and body.[1]

Think back to the impromptu speaking and ask yourself, "Is it true one hundred percent of the time that you are not a good singer or speaker?" No. You are smart and you do have a great deal of life experience from which to share and, if a singer, a good many songs to sing.

You now **choose** to have faith in your abilities, believe in yourself and God's power in you, and know you can do it. Now it is easy to "thank your brain for sharing the negative," but choose to ignore it, and replace it with the positive true thought. The negative thought then literally becomes hot air leaving your brain. Choose a true, good, and positive thought. Choose to replace the negative thought with a positive one that can be trusted (Bible Truth). Then the negative thought has become just a wisp of hot air and cannot return to the cortex and become a long-term damaging black hole of negative memory.

E + S = P is a formula I heard during one of the many insightful presentations I have listened to. E stands for an event and the S stands for your Story. The P represents the Problem or Perspective. The event may be you are on stage and you have a memory slip. What you choose to think about this event becomes your story. You can choose to allow it to be a negative story of panic and allow it to become a problem, or you can choose a positive "pregnant pause," a smile and make it work for you. No negative story means no problem.

E + negative ☹ S = ☹ Problem

E + positive ☺ story = ☺ Perspective and healthy thinking

Fear Versus Faith/Love:

> *"There is no fear in love. But perfect love drives out fear."* —1 John 4:18, (NIV)

You Were Created Out of Love for Love. Fear Is Learned. Your Default Is Love and Faith.

All emotions stem from these two, **faith** and **fear**. Loving faith-based thoughts are so much stronger than fear, even though fear can feel very strong when you are experiencing it. Faith will stabilize you, where fear shuts you down.

Fear:

When you feel a sudden jolt of fear, the brain secretes a harmful hormone dubbed the "negative emotion hormone" by doctors.

Suicide victims on autopsy show ten times more of this hormone present than the brains of people who die of natural causes. This hormone travels to other glands, then picks up more hormones that release cortisol and adrenaline.[1] This is not good news.

When these chemicals race unchecked through the body, they create adverse effects on your memory and cardiovascular system, causing high blood pressure, heart palpitations, aneurisms, and strokes. They also attack the immune system, diminishing its effectiveness. You were designed for short bursts of stress, not an avalanche of stress or on-going stress.[1]

Now when dealing with stage fright, remember that stage nerves are a mild form of the above process. **It is short lived and for your benefit**, when not allowed to become the great or long-term stress described above by negative thinking. **The adrenaline that pools when you feel stage nerves is there to ensure you will deliver your best work.** Think of this experience as stage **excitement** rather than fear of the stage. As you go on stage and begin to give your message or song to the audience, the "nerves" dissipate and you feel the adrenaline energy in your system and the joy of giving your gift to the audience. It isn't about you at that point. It is all about them, the audience. When it is over, you are "peeling yourself off the ceiling" with energy and joy for having delivered well. It always feels great to give a gift away, right?

The time to worry is when you **don't** feel stage nerves or excitement. **Remember that stage excitement or nerves are your best friends.** No matter how professional a person is or the length of time a person has performed, **everyone** feels stage nerves. The difference is the long-time professional knows the nerves are there to ensure success and are exciting!

Faith:

"I want to know God's thoughts; the rest are all details." —Einstein

"We live by faith, not by sight." —2 Corinthians 5:7, (NIV)

Knowing God's thoughts puts you on a path to faith, love, and healthy thinking, emotions, attitudes, body reactions, and behaviors. In short, faith puts you on a path to success as a speaker or singer. You must choose to live by faith, not by sight. It is said that seeing is believing. But the true power is in **choosing** to **believe** in order to **truly see** things differently and positively, and give a message of hope. Also, with faith, you don't have to worry about being tempted beyond your capacity to believe and succeed.

> *"No temptation has overtaken you except what is common to mankind. And God is faithful; he will not let you be tempted beyond what you can bear. But when you are tempted, he will also provide a way out so that you can endure it."* —1 Corinthians 10:13, (NIV)

For every negative thought and result, the converse is also true. When you experience faith, love, positive praise, recognition, and support, your brain and body release good chemicals to your body. Your cells and DNA are positively affected, and you experience more health, wellness, and delivery success. Your memory is also stronger and healthier, and you become more intelligent. Your intelligence actually can continue to develop and grow as you age.[1]

That is good news for you as a speaker or singer because it means you can continue to "present and shine with brilliance" and bless people for a very long time.

It was once thought that you were born with all of your brain capacity and that it could not be changed. Now the research shows a great plasticity of the brain to grow and change for the good or bad.[1] I encourage you toward the good. Faith and love keep you in the "Pink"!

When David faced Goliath, do you think he experienced fear? Yes! But he knew that the God of Israel, whom he was serving, would indeed "have his back." He even proclaimed to Goliath and all listening that it was not he, but his God, who would put Goliath down. And God did exactly that. David used his skill, ability, belief, and **faith** to kill Goliath and free Israel from the Philistines that day.

As stated before in a previous chapter, I used to be captive to a memory phobia of sorts. When I was on stage following Vonda Kay Vandyke, who became Miss America that year, I experienced a memory lapse and panicked. The experience frightened me, and I **fearfully** thought and determined I would not do anything again without a "cheat sheet" or method of self-prompting. Does this seem familiar to some of you? It followed me for several years.

Then, I **faithfully** thought, chose, and determined to allow the Holy Spirit to help me with words and memory. A very distinct memory previously shared of an incident on stage still thrills me:

When I was singing once, all of a sudden I was in panic mode and did not know the next word or phrase of the song. Keep in mind this all happened within a minuscule fraction of a second when I felt the panic and saw only red behind my eyes. Then I cried out to God in my mind in that same fraction of a second, and the Holy Spirit filled me with the words and all on time for the next musical entrance. I chose to trust with **faith** that the Holy Spirit of God would be there for me in all situations and rescue my thoughts on stage. He did and does faithfully every day.

Choosing to allow God's Spirit to help you and form thoughts in your mind is a powerful truth. I was tempted to be defeated with my toxic **panic** thinking, but my **choice** to faithfully trust God saved me and my memory. You will even amaze yourself at your God-given ability to recreate lyrics with the same meaning as the original lyrics when you don't remember the exact lyric.

Negative thoughts or panic bring darkness into your life. Positive thoughts of what you want brings light in. We are all "cracked pots." Those cracks are how light gets in. Look up and look for the light, God's light. Deep negativity feels like sharks are circling. Think positive thoughts like, "I like me and my smile." Celebrate yourself. It is as though birds are singing in your brain. Visualize happiness and light happens even brighter.

God created the way your spirit, mind, brain, and body work, and trusting Him and positive truth is always the best for success.

Your Heart Has a Brain, Your Last Chance to Take Charge

Many neuroscience researchers now believe that your heart actually contains around forty thousand brain neurons that speak directly to your "free will" in the frontal cortex. Yes, science has discovered genetic free will according to Dr. Leaf and others.

The frontal cortex is where your reasoning exists. What that means for you is when the Bible speaks of the heart, where God is speaking to you over nine hundred times, you reason it is good and right and receive the benefits. This bit of science makes sense and shows you how God speaks to you because of the way He created you. You have a capacity to hear Him and be able to reason well with God's information to you through your heart.

It is a scientific fact that you are a spiritual being attached to a body and brain. The spirit drives the mind. The mind drives the brain, and the brain drives the body. But they all interact with each other.[1,2]

I believe God has so created you to be able to hear from Him in this special heart-driven way. When you are calm and thinking healthily, you can hear God through your heart neurons talking to the reasoning part of the brain, specifically the free will in the frontal cortex. But if you are emotionally upset or thinking chaotically, you will not hear your heart at all. One way to know God's thoughts is to choose to be calm and listen to your heart and His Spirit speaking there. I find reading Scripture is a miracle for my spiritual ears to hear God's voice through my heart connection. But over the years, I have become good at hearing Him well at other times also.

In today's church practice of musical worship, a strong tendency exists to keep the driving beat and chaotic feel of the music high in intensity and volume for long periods of time. The result is that you, in the congregation or audience, cannot hear from your heart. God speaks to you through your heart neurons when you are in a calm state. You cannot and do not hear from Him adequately during that kind of chaotic worship. As a musician and lover of God, this grieves me deeply.

There is a reason God inspired the musical greats, such as Bach, Handel, and others, to write for the church to truly honor and offer praise to Himself. Bach's music and that of most of the Baroque, Classical, and Romantic music eras was melodic, interesting, soothing, and **not** chaotic. It was easy to listen to, and God could speak through it to your heart. It was also at times greatly exciting and majestic as in Handel's Messiah.

When you want people to open up, be creative, and inspired, you have them listen to music from the Baroque musical period, where the beat and melodic lines were of a calmer consistent meter with a beautifully calming feel. The brain science has proven over and over the good effects of this style of music on the brain and body.

Now, I am not saying we need to play only Baroque music in church. What I am saying is, if you want to truly worship and hear fully from God, you must *be still and know that He is God* in the process of worship. Bring the chaos down to a calm level enough to be able to hear from Him as you worship in song. And, wouldn't it be a wonderful thing to expose our youth to some of their Christian heritage of music and hymns once in a while and accomplish not only hearing God's heart, but give the gift of musical heritage to our youth!

"Be still and know that I am God" —Psalms 46:10, (NIV)

God has your best in mind, and your heart brain is your last important chance to check your attitude. It is where you can tap into your spirit, the Holy Spirit of God, and not only your good judgment, but your **best** judgment.

Build Up Your Brain Power

"There is a God-shaped hole or vacuum in the heart of every man that cannot be filled by any created thing, but only by God, the Creator, made known through Jesus Christ."—Blaise Pascal, French mathematician, physicist, philosopher (1623–1662) (taken from works of Augustine)

> *"For the word of God is living and active and full of power [making it operative, energizing, and effective]. It is sharper than any two-edged sword, penetrating as far as the division of the soul and spirit [the completeness of a person], and of both joints and marrow [the deepest parts of our nature], exposing and judging the very thoughts and intentions of the heart."*—**Hebrews 4:12 (AMP)**

The best news of all is that no matter what you have experienced, with God's help you can stop, take control, and improve your brain function, which will positively affect your life and speaking or singing success. Learn to apply the following steps taken from Dr. Caroline Leaf and my own research:

1. Understand how important your thoughts are to your overall well-being and speaking success.
2. Be alert and aware of your thoughts and the emotions expressed in your body. Never react to your first strong

emotion. Stand back and analyze instead. Express your emotions calmly and healthily—not bottling them up. All emotions, positive or negative, become toxic and harmful when bottled up or blocked. The roots of bitterness and unforgiveness can destroy you.

3. Take every thought captive by using your intellect and attitude check points:

    •   Your God-given intellect sieve of **awareness** (where have I seen or heard this before?)

    •   How does it feel in my body?

    •   Choice and will (ask, answer, and discuss with yourself, and choose to put a positive spin on your thought)

    •   Allow God to assure you of His presence and power in your heart, thoughts, and in your powerfully chosen actions.

4. Protect what comes into your brain through your senses, especially what you see and hear. Be careful about how much time you spend with computer screens and devices. Too much media time can alter your brain negatively.[2]

5. Choose your thoughts purposefully. Scriptural, positive "can do" thinking is healthy and feels great. Always replace negative excuses with positive faith and love-based thoughts. Excuses are usually rationalizations for keeping rotten thoughts, and rotten thoughts will "take you out." Take responsibility and control. Remember, *"All things are possible with God.*—Matthew 19:26; Mark 10:27, (NIV)

6. Speak words out loud to frame your world, because there are electromagnetic properties in your words, as well as the power to heal or harm you and others. What you say out

loud feeds back to your brain and body. This is great news for a speaker. Watch your self-talk. Speak love and positive truth to yourself and about yourself.

7. Use your thinker. Ask, answer, and discuss everything with yourself. Ask if it is true one hundred percent of the time? As you use both sides of your brain, be sure you are not making excuses or rationalizations for harmful thinking and behavior. No victim mentality or negative thinking — victims never win!

8. Accept uplifting emotional thoughts and reject negative ones. Focus on what you want — not on what you do not want.

9. Live in the NOW, or present. It is a gift, thus called the **present**. By the way, the present is where you will experience God. His presence is a fifth dimension to be added to the four dimensions we know as: 1. time, and space which incorporates 2. height, 3. width, and 4. depth.

10. Contemplate good and meditate on God's words of positive affirming truth. Since you are a spiritual being in a body controlled by a mind, get to know your Creator, for He created you and loves you. Soak in calm music and listen to your heart. You will hear from Him there.

11. Be passionate. Passion is a healthy motivator and promoter of positive healthy thinking. Dream on! Your "ideal world" thinking will bring your brain alive, hopeful, creative, and active.

12. Be compassionate. Love and faith are the most powerful and healthy forces in the world. Thoughts make you well or sick. It is your choice.

13. Think forgiveness. Beware of the root of bitterness forming in your root system. Forgive and keep trusting God. Lack of forgiveness is like drinking poison, hoping the other guy dies. Keep your roots of mind, and body clean and healthy. That way bitterness cannot take hold of you.

14. Love, hug, play, and laugh a lot. Life is ninety percent mental and only ten percent physical. Your body projects your thoughts and mental energy.

15. Exercise and drink half your body weight in ounces of water daily. Eat healthily, relax, and sleep at least eight hours a night. Remember, your body feeds your brain and creates good brain chemistry. Take care of your body and brain. It is said that your DNA is the gun, but your lifestyle of eating and thinking pulls the trigger!

My hope is that this chapter will whet your appetite and encourage you to take charge and learn more about your amazing spirit, mind, and body connection. Remember, it is possible and important to truly think your way to health, happiness, and success—all key ingredients that help create an amazing voice and Presenting with Brilliance!

Chapter 7

OWNER-SHIP OF YOUR BODY AND VOICE

"Don't you realize that your body is a temple of the Holy Spirit, who lives in you and was given to you by God? You do not belong to yourself."

—1 Corinthians 6:19, (NIV)

Vocal application: *Voice is very physical whether you are speaking or singing. The actual vocal production system, support system, and language are all physically based in your body. Taking care of the body with good air, water, nutrition, exercise, and rest are all important to how effective you are as a speaker and singer. You must take care of the body that houses your voice and brain. Remember the mind and body roots deal with your relationship with yourself and God. All vocal success reflects back to this relationship with yourself and your Maker.*

T
o further understand the tree analogy, you must understand, as previously stated, that you are a triune person (spirit, mind, and body) and that your voice is also a triune system. Voice is first a **physical** system of muscles and connective responses from the body. Second, it is a **mental** system of thoughts, attitudes, and beliefs. And third, voice is a **spiritual** system that allows your God-given purpose and passion to come through your Holy Spirit-infused spirit out to others to bless them. Remember, your spirit drives the mind, which drives the brain, and the brain drives your body.

There are three specialized systems of the voice: (1) sound production; (2) sound support; and (3) language (understanding how to produce clear and understandable language). These three systems are all affected by the spirit, mind, and body.

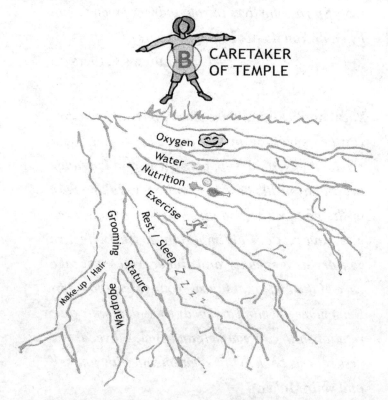

B — CARETAKER OF TEMPLE

Oxygen
Water
Nutrition
Exercise
Rest / Sleep
Grooming
Make-up / Hair
Wardrobe
Stature

Let's look at how each area affects you and your voice. First, let's look at the physical side of voice. You are the OWNER of your body, and everything that you do to care for your body affects your physical voice.

> *"Do you not know that your body is the temple of the Holy Spirit who is in you, whom you have received from God, and you are not your own? For you were bought at a price; therefore glorify God with your bodies."* — 1 Corinthians 6:19–20, (NKJV)

That means you must take care of your body because God's Spirit lives inside you. He even calls your body His temple, so it is very important to respect, love, and take great care of your amazing body. He has made you OWNER and caretaker of His temple while on this planet. It is not a suggestion, but a command from God.

O in OWNER stands for OXYGEN. The quality of the air you breathe has a healthy or destructive effect on your voice; in fact, your whole being. When the air you breathe is clean and not polluted with smoke or other toxins, your lungs and vocal cords are free to perform well. Asthma is primarily an allergic inflammatory condition and often is accompanied by a cough. The pollutants in the air contribute to this effect. Coughing slams together the vocal cords badly and creates hoarseness in the voice. I have struggled with a croupy asthma cough for years and have had to overcome the ill effects of it with vocal technique and understanding how to use my voice healthily. As a result, I am still singing well. Helping other asthmatics learn to open up and breathe healthily, as in vocal support, has been a blessing. What a joy to be able to help improve the lives of others with the God-given experiential understanding of being asthmatic, and the years of great vocal training I have been blessed to have experienced.

Do everything in your power to control the cough and breathe healthy clean air. Pray for God's healing and help. God has answered my prayers in helping me get off the inhalers that were causing some of my voice issues. The inhalers have been altering my vocal cords for years, making it difficult to sing my full vocal range. I asked God to help me find a solution, and He delivered an answer through two herbal products that help my lungs and vocal cords, or folds, as well. These supplements have worked better for me than the inhalers I was on for so many years, although a new inhaler seems to be working well for me now along with my herbal supplements. You will find more information at the back of this book in the bibliography section.

W in OWNERS stands for WATER. The amount of clean unpolluted water you take in daily helps your vocal cords operate well. Your whole being, body and brain, needs water desperately. Your body is about seventy-five to eighty-five percent water, and your brain is as much as ninety to ninety-five percent water. Water is vital to your total well-being and balance of weight, energy, and healthy bodily functions, including your voice. A great rule is to drink half your body weight in ounces of water. If you weigh one hundred and fifty pounds, you will want to drink seventy-five ounces of water per day. It helps to drink five sixteen ounce glasses or bottles, rather than ten eight ounce glasses. If you start with your first glass on rising, it becomes much easier to get your water in twenty-four hours. Remember, you must drink water and must exclude counting in coffee, tea, or any other drinks. Keep juices at a minimum and

no sodas. Soda drinks have no value and are actually detrimental to your health and voice.

N stands for NUTRITION. We all are inundated with information on nutrition. I am personally a huge fan of Dr. Mehmet Oz.[3] He has done a great deal to educate the American public on the benefits of good healthy nutrition, thus helping to expel the confusion that is so prevalent. Nutrition also affects the health of the voice. Proper organic protein, veggies, fruit, healthy unprocessed grains, legumes, and fats are needed for cell production, energy, and weight balance. Being overweight can have an ill effect on the breathing and vocal production and general overall health also.

In order to identify protein, ask yourself if the food source once walked, swam, or flew. If so, or if by-products come from it, it is protein. If it grows from seed or bulb, it is a carbohydrate. And it is a good fat if it is a plant source, such as olives, almonds, walnuts, coconut oil, or avocado. So many fats in our diets are highly processed and **not** healthy even if they come from some plant sources, such as canola or corn.

A great way to use good nutrition to your best benefit is to eat breakfast with at least twenty-five grams of protein within the first half hour of rising in the morning. Then eat a balanced snack of one or two ounces of organic protein, apple, or veggie of choice. Lunch and dinner would be a smaller plate with protein to equal the flat of your open hand minus your fingers (one third your plate), and green healthy vegetables for the other two-thirds of the plate. Before dinner include an afternoon snack of one ounce protein with fruit or veggie. Your grains can be taken with vegetables at dinner, but with no protein at that meal, as mixing grain carbohydrates and protein cause the meal to be stagnate and ferment in your digestive tract. Things to avoid are putting protein with grains or starches at the same meal. Fruit is best on an empty stomach. Anything white is usually not good for you and should be avoided (white processed breads, white potatoes, and rice, etc.)

What I know to be true is that today's wheat products produce sensitivities in many people because wheat has been modified and is not the same as it was fifty years ago, when we tolerated it better. Please read Dr. William Davis's book, *Wheat Belly Total Health* to get another great perspective.[3] Dairy products, such as milk, cheese and yogurts, are another problem food for many singers, speakers, and people in general.

You must eat well and keep your weight and health in good shape to be at your best. I have just given you some basic tips, but there is a plethora of nutrition information available to you. Research a bit more to find what works best for you and your body. (See Bibliography, Dr. Mehmet Oz[3] and Dr. William Davis[3]).

E stands for EXERCISE and ENERGY. The more you are willing to get moving, the better your brain and body work for you. Memorizing lyrics and thinking clearly for great speaking delivery get better when you exercise and are grounded in your body through movement. Thirty minutes a day of walking is great exercise for the brain and produces a wealth of benefits for the body.

R stands for REST. Eight hours of sleep at night or more is crucial for healthy cellular repair and detoxification. Your weight control depends on this sleep as well. You speak and sing best when you are well rested. Too much sleep, as in ten hours or more, has a negative effect on your overall efficiency. Often, when we think we need more rest, we may really need a little protein or glass of water.

The other parts of the physicality of voice involve good grooming habits and stature (see chapter 9). Your posture and how you carry yourself says a great deal about you before you say a word. When you know how to put yourself together to represent yourself well, by dressing fashionably and standing with body confidence and good grounding, you will look and feel confident. Your physical body affects your mental state, and your mental state affects your body.

Chapter 8

LET'S GET PHYSICAL WITH VOICE

"Make a joyful (noise) shout to the Lord, all you lands! Serve the Lord with gladness; come before His presence with singing. Know that the Lord, He is God; It is He who has made us, and not we ourselves; we are His people and the sheep of His pasture. Enter into His gates with thanksgiving, and into His courts with praise. Be thankful to Him, and bless His name. For the Lord is good; His mercy is everlasting, and His truth endures to all generations." **—Psalm 100, (NKJV)**

Vocal application: *God has given us all a voice to be used for His glory. When He says, "Make a joyful noise or shout," the word "noise" refers to the lovely joyful sound your human voice makes when you are authentically praising or engaged. It isn't noise, or dissonant sounds, as we think of* *today. Everyone can sing, and I have proven that many times in my studio. People that had the desire to sing, but were told they could not, actually transformed and became lovely singers. Some went on to sing in church choirs and worship groups. Some went on to do pageant work and won titles and crowns. Just as we all can sing, we all can speak well with clarity and authentic intention of heart through a beautiful broadcast system called voice. Also, God allows creative connections to other speakers and singers in our lives to encourage us. I love certain singers and speakers, and as a result, they influence my voice in a good way. In fact, some people say I sound like some of them at times.*

Physical Vocal System:

N ow let's look at the physical vocal system, the sound-producing mechanism. Your voice is a two-"horned" instrument. The sound coming though those two "horns," or pharynges, is what phonation is all about.

Picture a trumpet. You have a perfectly formed constant horn. Now blow with proper lip position, and support from your diaphragm muscle, and out comes a lovely sound. But, put that same trumpet horn down and drive a huge truck across it. What happens to the horn? Yes, it is smashed, altered, or closed. Try to blow through it with the same good consistent lip position and same support. What do you get? An altered sound because the shape of the horn is altered.

Your voice is a two-horned instrument that must be open and maintained when you speak or sing. Those two horns, or pharynges, are very flexible and constantly changing their shape. They are the oral pharynx, and the nasal pharynx.

They don't automatically stay open and wonderful like the trumpet horn. You must know how to open them and maintain openness to be able to phonate a clear and resonating sound. In the above example of the trumpet, the vocal cords represent your mouth position, which is consistent, and your support to blow is the same for trumpet and voice.

The sound-producing mechanism is composed of muscles that you need to identify and strengthen. In addition, there are some muscles that need to be be identified and consciously relaxed (out of the way) in order for your horns to remain open.

We all have opposite sets of muscles in our bodies called constrictors and their opposites, the anti-constrictors. Try to smile and pucker up or purse your lips at the same time. You will experience the effect of the opposing nature of "smile" muscles versus the "pucker" muscles. The smile represents openness, or in the case of voice, throat and palate opening muscles, which open the oral and nasal pharynges. The pucker represents the constricting action of throat closing muscles.

95

Open your hands and spread your fingers.

Now make a fist.

The open out-stretched hand represents anti-constrictors, like the ones that open your throat. The fist represents the constrictors that close your throat. If you did not know, you would think the same set of muscles create both actions. But the truth is, there are two sets of muscles that lie side by side to create the opposite actions.

The constrictor muscles constrict or tighten and close the throat to protect you. They produce the gag, the cough, and the swallow, etc.

The anti-constrictors open you up and produce the yawn and the throat opening responses. The image below shows the soft palate, teeth, the open oral pharynx, the tongue, and the tonsils, all of which are influenced by strong anti-constrictors and constrictors in the system.

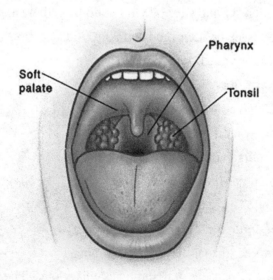

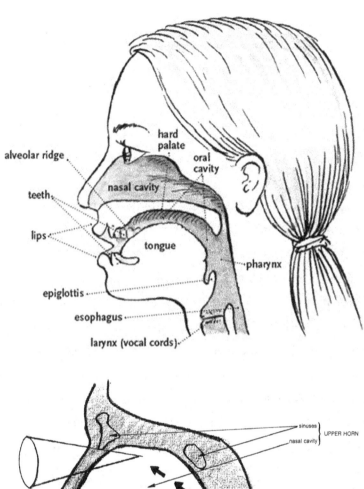

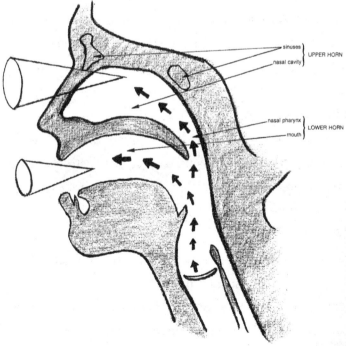

In the next images, you will see the upper horn, lower horn, the nasal cavity and pharynx. You will also see the oral pharynx and more closed oral cavity, because the tongue is in a more constrictive position. The upper lip and soft palate control the openness of the upper nasal horn, or pharynx, while the tongue and associated muscles that create the yawn control the lower oral horn, or pharynx.

The key to getting in touch with the conscious effect of these "good guy" anti-constricor muscles, is to identify and strengthen the anti-constrictors in your throat and tongue in order to maximize openness. Then learn to identify and relax away the constrictor muscles that close your vocal phonation. When you consciously relax the constrictors in singing or speaking, you encourage great openness. And you experience deeper body relaxation, as your stress response happens in the throat area first over any other part of the body. As you learn to deeply relax the constrictors in the tongue, you feel an immediate deep upper body relaxation as well. With this wonderful ability to relax vocal constrictors, you discover hidden or suppressed stressors. Then you learn to identify the hidden stressor thoughts, bring them to consciousness, release them, allow them to rest with Jesus, and experience your body let go of them as well. There is no danger of negatively affecting the benefits to you of the constrictors muscles as reflexive protectors, as in swallowing or coughing, etc.

Now, open and spread your fingers and then, while keeping your fingers spread, begin to make a fist. You cannot keep your hand open when a fist-making action is engaged and in the way. **The important information here is that you want to be strong in your ability to activate your anti-contrictors, or throat opening**

muscles, in order to open up and not have the constrictors fighting you by pulling you in a closing direction.

Also, the vocal cords need to be healthy. One can drink and breathe steam from warm to hot liquids and water to help the cords perform well. There are a number of old wives' tales about eating or drinking certain things for the voice. What I know for sure is that the vocal cords need to be hydrated, and water in your system is the best for that. As mentioned in chapter 7, drink at least one half your body weight in ounces of water daily. Keep sodas and carbonated liquids to a minimum. Menthol is not good for vocal folds or cords, and reflux acid is also very damaging. Post nasal drainage also takes a toll on vocal cords. Getting enough rest and eating smaller meals to avoid reflux is just good common sense when it comes to voice. Lemon in water is good, as it has an alkalizing effect on the body and thus the vocal cords.

Vocal cords open during breathing to allow air into lungs.

Vocal cords close when speaking so air from the lungs presses between them to cause the vibrations that produce sound.

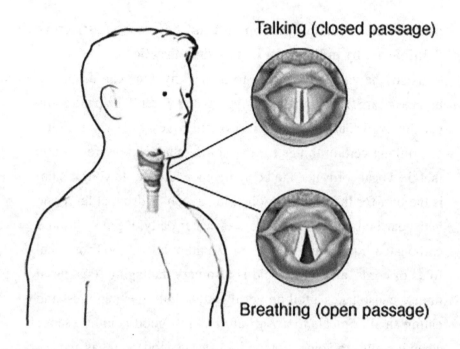

Talking (closed passage)

Breathing (open passage)

Your mind is a huge part of the physical process, because you must believe you can consciously control your muscles well. Your belief system enables or shuts down success. To be successful, an athlete needs mental toughness. That means being mentally strong and careful about what he or she thinks. Read chapter 6 for greater insight and understanding of the mind and brain.

There is more to vocal success than this, and more muscles to master, but the beginning of identifying, understanding, and strengthening the phonation space in your two-horned instrument is a vital beginning step. There is an oral pharynx and a nasal pharynx, and both need to be understood, strengthened, and open for good phonation. Focusing on the inner vocal game makes control possible. When you sense fear, you can overcome it with faith and physical knowledge in your ability to open and stay open. This gives you the confidence that your voice will always be there for you when you have to sing or speak to an audience. Sound produced when you are truly open, and strong in that openness, creates a special **feeling** of sound. Open tones feel great and resonate in a beautiful way inside your head. You get used to physically opening in order to feel beautifully produced sound, and thus, you are confident with or without any microphone or amplification.

A quick note on using a microphone. It is best to hold the microphone gently on a forty-five degree angle with finger versus a whole hand grip close to the mouth. Hold it close enough that if it was an ice-cream cone held at an angle, you could lick it easily.

You need individual coaching to learn this total vocal production process, and I am available to help you. See the contact information at the back of this book. Remember, many wonderful and well-meaning voice teachers or coaches were not trained in this physiology of voice, and they may not understand this amazing process. I am here to help you and them as well.

The sound-supporting mechanism and language are also equally important to good vocal production. But if you master the phonation or sound-producing mechanism first, then the other systems are much more easily mastered as well. This is true because muscles work with other muscles in a certain way, and mastering phonation skills ensures success in your breathing techniques and vowel/consonant relationship as well. Then you will experience the God-given coordination of **all** vocal systems and truly know how it feels to speak or sing through your open, free, and expressive voice.

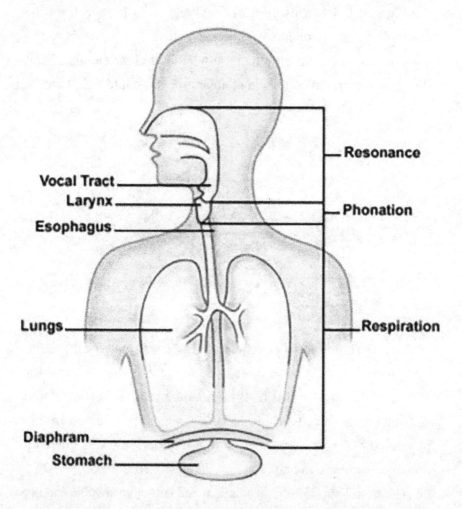

The support system depends on constrictors and anti-constrictors working in opposition of each other to create compression, much like a compressed paint spray gun. Have you ever yelled at a dog or cat out of frustration with their behavior? Did you worry about breath support? No! You just got the job done without thinking. When you identify low lung breathing and strengthen that response away from singing, so as to be more automatic all the time, the support system will work correctly and well, with the open two-horned sound producing system phonating and leading the way. There are wonderful connections with the muscles in both systems that ensure success with support when the open throat muscles are in play. It is important to focus on phonation production to free the support system.

You never want to focus totally on support while you are speaking or singing because muscles trigger muscles. Remember, the constrictors are throat closing muscles, and because muscles trigger muscles, you don't want to be triggering a smile-pucker response in the sound-producing system while thinking about support. Your focus must be on openness and anti-constrictors, and then the support will kick in appropriately for you. This fact cuts down vocal mastery time considerably because your mental-physical focus is clear and correct, up in the sound phonation system where your quality and quantity are controlled. You focus and build the support system away from singing and speaking, so it supports you automatically when you open to speak or sing.

Language is a fascinating and intriguing system. You can only really speak or sing well on vowel sounds (the sounds the words create). The vowels resonate and fill the room with sound. The consonants are the percussive connectors for the vowels. When you understand this wonderful effective vowel-consonant relationship and delivery process, your ability to be heard and understood clearly by your audience improves dramatically. There is a rule that says: "There is no such thing as an end consonant." Consonants only begin things. If a consonant ends a syllable or word, it is to be chopped off and shoved over to the beginning of the new vowel in the syllable or word. For instance, "Mary had a little lamb" would look like this: Mareee ha dah lih tuh la mb. The **d** of **had** is moved to begin **a**, and **little** is now **li tuh** with the **l** of the word, little, sounding with the **l** of lamb. The **mb** of lamb is moved or pushed into another word or into the breath. This process frees the vowel sound to stay open and move to the next vowel sound unhampered. Words and syllables are well understood because the vowels are free and the consonants are crisp and perfectly placed.

Another important element of great speaking or singing is the use of the body as an expressive tool. As stated before, the rule of seven percent applies. Your words are only seven percent of your total communication. Ninety-three percent of communication is in how you are thinking, in body, and voice tone. There is *"power in the tongue to curse or bless,"* and there is power in the body to express and caress in a safe and loving way, or not. We can slap or strike out and create fear, or we can caress and create safety and love.

Remember, when you are speaking, the use of your hands as extensions of your arms moving space around you is an extension of your emotion, as well as an expression of your heart. You caress the air around you, or strongly move air, as you gesture with gentleness or power. It is never about moving an arm or hand. It is about expressing genuine emotion through moving space around you with your gesture, extending energy out through your limbs as a dancer does. Standing grounded and tall allows you to extend your arms and move your body in meaningful ways when speaking. I will cover stature and grounding in the next chapter. Again, coaching helps you understand all this better.

Eye contact is another very important part of speaking. You must never look over or above your audience, but directly at them. Find many sets of eyes to connect with, one set at a time. This way you are speaking to one person at a time and really connecting with people, heart to heart. Your effectiveness and credibility depend on you being authentic in every way. Your eyes are the windows to your soul that reflect and demonstrate your genuine intent and authentic purposeful energy.

As stated before, it is best to receive coaching through all of these processes. My passion is to do so and truly help you achieve the greatness you desire. Because of technology we can work from anywhere in the world. Please contact me and allow me to be of service to you.

Here are a few great transformation stories: I remember two lovely women who came to me for help. They were told they could not sing and to please not sing because they sang off-key, or out of tune and pitch. After working with me, they not only sang, but sang on pitch, and joined their church worship group.

Another great story is of a young high school student who was a dancer and was auditioning for her school choir. She wanted to sing and was told she was not a singer, and not to bother. She came to me and asked if I could help her. I was beginning to use a new physiological method, so I asked her if she was willing to give the whole process a try. She said yes and we began working together. In a matter of months she was singing well and entered a local Miss America pageant. She took first runner-up as a singer. The winner went on to the state Miss America pageant, and first runner-up went on to the Miss Seafair Pageant, which was a huge scholarship pageant at the time. She wanted to dance and sing, but someone told her it was not a good idea. I told her, "Of course, you can sing and dance. Let me show you how." We choreographed her song with a corded microphone, as we were not guaranteed of having a cordless microphone at the time. Guess what? She took the crown and won a sizable scholarship and traveled as representative of her city to their sister city in Japan and elsewhere in the world. How is that for the success of a girl who was told she was not a singer! I hate to think what would have happened if she had believed her school choral teacher, and not pursued the dream in her heart.

Many students have left my studio and gone on to university to find their vocal skills serving them well. A few have come back to me a bit frustrated because of experiencing a university music professor with different terminology of "chest versus head voice" and other terms. The chest voice versus head voice sets up a mental separation, as if there were two different voices. It only takes a short session with me to set them back on their feet of understanding the professor's terms in a way that relates to the true physiology and what is true about voice. It is one beautiful voice with connected registers. When given phonation space as discussed earlier in open muscle structure, the voice finds its own place and is heady, and it can be chesty as well throughout the whole voice. There is no true separation, only registers that roll in and out of each other. **When done correctly, there is no break in the voice.**

One of my speaking clients came to me desiring to speak without fear. She was beginning a new business and wanted to share her passion with many audiences. She was a delight to work with as we developed her voice and message, and helped her own it and deliver it with great passion from her heart. As she began really giving her gift to the audience, she found her fear levels changed into excitement, which empowered her to deliver well. In fact, she went on to do keynote addresses to many organizations. It is always about your audience and the gift you bring to them. It is not about you or concerns for yourself.

The last story I will share here is of a wonderful young man with Down's syndrome. He loved to sing, but he was driving his family a bit crazy with his constant singing of one pitch, either very loud or soft, to any song he was trying to sing. I had met his mother at a fund-raiser, and she asked if I could help her son. We got together and I succeeded in getting him to match two or three notes on the piano. We began working together, and he went from two or three notes to nearly three full octaves. He was singing with thirty-seven to thirty-nine notes! And he was singing songs with orchestration accompaniment and in key and pitch.

It is very common for a vocal student to think they can only sing low, and then discover a wide and wonderful range of high and low notes. Most people can learn to sing anything they desire. The phonation for a speaker is the same as for a singer, but many times people do not get help with this. Your quality and quantity both come from knowing how to achieve great phonation space with the voice. The support kicks in naturally when phonation space is used correctly. We simply develop them separately and allow the wonderful way God designed them to work take over.

Finding the **sweet spot** of your voice involves your thought management, your vocal horn management, and your body management, all beautifully coordinated and functioning in concert.

Speakers need to know all that is discussed for singers. They just don't take the phonation skills quite as far as a singer does, because speaking range of variance isn't as wide as singing. Although, I do get my speakers to sing a bit to help them understand better all the phonation, support, and language skills necessary in speaking or singing.

Chapter 9

YOUR WRAPPING SPEAKS VOLUMES

"Charm and grace are deceptive, and (superficial) beauty is vain. But a woman who fears the Lord (reverently worshiping, obeying, serving, and trusting Him with awe-filled respect), she shall be praised." **—Proverbs 31:30,** (AMP)

"I also want the women to dress modestly, with decency and propriety, adorning themselves, not with elaborate hairstyles or gold or pearls or expensive clothes, but with good deeds, appropriate for women who profess to worship God." **—1 Timothy 2:9-10,** (NIV)

Vocal Application: *Beauty comes from within and how you choose to think, or express your attitude. As a man or woman thinks in his or her heart, so* *is he or she. But how you carry yourself with posture and stature, how you dress and present physically with proper grooming and wardrobe, and total demeanor is critical to your over-all success as a speaker or singer. Modesty with elegance and refinement show you know who you are, respect yourself, respect your audience, and have something of value to share. Elaborate, overly expensive, sexy, gaudy, or grungy casual appearance is not appropriate for a professional, because it will say to your audience you really do not honor them or yourself.*

What Does It Mean To Be Professional?

The Free Dictionary.com by Farlex, Inc. 2016, version 7 says: being a professional "pertains to one relating to, engaged in, or suitable for a profession; conforming to the standards of a profession, as in professional behavior; engaging in a given activity as a source of livelihood or as a career; a person following a profession, especially a learned profession; one who earns a living in a given or implied occupation; a skilled practitioner; an expert; a person who engages for his livelihood in some activity also pursued by amateurs.

In addition to the dictionary definitions, we often associate professional with a person who engages in constant practice of something to become an expert, like a skill or dressing to demand respect of self and others.

You must ask yourself what message you send others as you endeavor to be professional. You want to be an expert speaker or singer whom others desire to listen to, right? So, what are you saying with your whole demeanor? What you wear, how you wear it, how you do your hair and use make-up, how you groom yourself, and what attitude you display all reflect your demeanor.

I must share a story here of how a beautiful woman morphed into ugly before my very eyes. I once showed up for a modeling job and reported to my petite models' area. On my way, I passed by the tall models' area. I observed a drop-dead gorgeous model and could not take my eyes off her. As I listened to her talk with another tall and beautiful model, I experienced a dramatic phenomena. The two physically beautiful women began to morph from lovely and beautiful to harsh, cold, and uncaring women who became actually unlovely and worse than ugly. Their appearance became incongruent with what they were saying, and their physical beauty was totally undermined by their ugly attitudes, which destroyed their beauty in my eyes. All of a sudden they were not so physically beautiful.

You must take seriously the power of congruency of attitude and love, reflected through your best efforts to take care of your mind and body, allowing your spirit to eminate out and communicate well. I have also experienced men and women who could be described as Plain Janes and Jims become beautiful and handsome. Because of the beauty of their spirits and minds, their bodies morphed into being lovely before my eyes.

At first glance, the second scripture at the beginning of this chapter can seem intimidating to us in this modern world of fashion and beauty. But as we understand the deeper meaning, we see that the advice is sound and applies to today in effective ways.

Wardrobe Is Important

In order to look and present your best, you must know how to dress to flatter your body to create a polished look and slimming illusion. Avoid horizontal lines, especially across the chest area or any other part of the body you want to minimize. You must understand basic design. Use of vertical lines or V shapes in your dress creates longer lines and thus slims your body appearance. It is never appropriate to use skirts with hemlines any higher than above the knee. Mid-knee hemlines are the most flattering.

Low-cut tops or short tops that reveal midriff skin are never appropriate for women. Pants or slacks are best, with straight legs from the hip to give you a longer, leaner look. These slim and flatter the hips. The current tight-legged pants are not very flattering on most men and women, and should be avoided in favor of a more moderately slim pant. Use of cardigans and jackets provide a finishing touch and helps to pull an outfit and overall look together. When purchasing clothes, always buy sizes that fit the largest part of you, and tailor the rest to fit. Use color, texture, print, and shine in your clothing choices for interest and professionalism.

In our culture there is an emphasis on looking "sexy" or provocative. After interviewing young men and older men, the consensus they shared is that a woman who dresses with modesty and illusion is much more desirable than one who dresses provocatively. In this day and age of sexual misconduct and sexual harassment, it is best to be aware that men are stimulated visually toward sexual thoughts and activity much more than women. So be aware and dress modestly in good taste. Many women want to wear provocative clothing and then wonder why they are treated with disrespect or harassment. I love to refer to the Biblical story of Esther to illustrate this.

It took twelve months of special beauty treatments and training to prepare Esther in order to appear before the king. She was dressed beautifully and modestly when presented to him. Keep in mind, he had many concubines in his harem he could call upon anytime he so chose. He had all the "sexiness" he wanted 24/7. What he wanted for his queen was different. He wanted beauty, refinement, and respectfulness versus a more provocative dress and behavior.

What Do You Want?

Do you want to be seen as a desirable "queen" who respects herself and has great information and presentation to better the world? Or do you want to project lack of self-respect, cluelessness about professionalism, and not be heard for who you really are and what you have to share? **Remember, people only give you approximately five seconds to determine if they want to know you or listen to you and what you have to say.**

Men need to pay attention to how they dress as well. They need to always be groomed, clean, and professionally dressed when speaking or singing. Make sure your clothes fit and are not too large or too small. Suits are always appropriate. Hair should be well trimmed as well as any facial hair. Clean shaven is best, but if you choose to sport a beard, be sure it is well trimmed and shaped to flatter your face. Beards that are not groomed and trimmed push people away from you. They indicate to others you don't care how you appear. Well-trimmed beards draw people toward you. If you look good, you feel good.

There is a saying that is always true: "Dress one notch higher than your general audience out of respect for them." Today we go to concerts and experience entertainers in cut-out or cut-off jeans, T-shirts, and with a grungy appearance. But I guarantee you that if you try that sort of appearance as a speaker or singer in the professional world, they will not take you seriously at all. They will be distracted by your appearance, won't hear what you have to say, and will feel dishonored by you. Even if you are a "rocker" type, please respect your whole audience by dressing "up" from your general audience. Wear a really nice shirt and dark wash jeans or slacks, with a vest and perhaps a tie. You have great influence to improve the world's attitudes and behaviors, so use it well!

Again, What Are You Saying with Your Appearance?

Another important detail of appearance is to be sure nothing you are wearing becomes a distraction to the audience. When you are on stage, be sure the view from the audience is a good one. I observed a lovely woman on stage, and all I could see, from my position in the audience, was her round tummy in her red slacks. Her tummy became a distraction because it was overly visible. I did not hear all she was saying because I was distracted and thinking of how she could have looked much better with a few fixes of her outfit for stage. When speaking to her when we were on the same eye level, her outfit looked passably fine, but on stage her outfit was not appropriate, as it showed too much, and more than she bargained for when she dressed that morning.

Another instance was a lovely young woman speaking at a business conference. I kept seeing something hanging off her hem. It became a huge distraction to what she was sharing with the audience. At the break I offered to trim off her dangling threads, and she became terribly upset at the thought of me trimming her hem. She had paid a lot of money for this "raveling" designer dress and was not okay with my offer of a trim job. Well, my advice is not to wear your expensive "raveling" designer dress for stage appearances or any appearance where people can see the ravel, but not the reason for the ravel, and be distracted by your hemline. In close proximity, where it is apparent that you are wearing a knit designed to ravel, it can work. Generally speaking, most audiences are too far away to recognize a designer ravel over a string hanging off your hem!

These are just two examples of distractions that can negatively affect your audience. If your shirt or blouse is unkempt, open, or too low, your appearance becomes distracting. Be sure dresses, skirts, slacks or trousers are in good shape and fit well—not too tight. All belts and shoes should be in good condition, clean, and polished. Be sure you are clean with a mild perfume or aftershave. Sometimes, the senses are overwhelmed by too much perfume, jewelry, huge hair, masking make-up, unkempt clothes, or untrimmed beards, etc. These are all distractions to the audience and keep them from seeing the real you and being interested in what you came to share. Something you can do is have a friend sit on the floor and look up at you to help you understand what may be a stage distraction. Or you can tilt a door or floor mirror such that it helps you see on an upward angle, showing you a similar view of how your audience sees you on stage.

Let's Look at Grooming, Hair and Make-up.

You always want to be healthy with clean skin, hair, and clothes. Hairstyles should always frame your face and bring attention to your eyes. They are the windows to your soul and reveal the deeper you. Always look your audience in the eyes. Eye contact is vital as a speaker or singer. It allows your authenticity to show.

Be sure your hair does not hide your face or eyes. Today's styles tend to leave a lot of hair in the face, so be sure you have modified your hairdo or anchored your bangs out of your face with appropriate hair products. You will be stylish, but effective, if your face and eyes are not hidden behind a face full of flopping hair!

Use make-up to enhance what God did right all along. Never use make-up to mask or hide behind. Think about what you looked like as a young child. You had clear eyes and skin with pink lips and cheeks. So, clear smooth skin with soft cheek color on apples of cheeks is appropriate and flattering. Eye make-up is best with natural eye shadows in the creases the way you had as a child. Avoid colors such as blues and greens for eye shadows. Pinkish bronze is good on most women, as it reflects natural shadow colors and areas. Most women need a light vanilla on lids to bring them forward and shadow in the crease above the lid. Eye liner applied deep in the bases of lashes and mascara finish the look. Use a reflective highlighter in the corners of the eyes and just under the arch of the eyebrow. Be sure eyebrows are groomed, shaped well to your face, and filled in. As we get older, the lashes and brows thin, so fuller brows and lashes are age flattering to you.

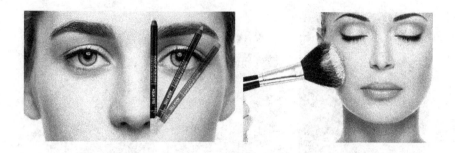

Be sure brows and shadows never extend beyond the eye area. Take a pencil and place it beside your nose and corner of eye. Brows and shadows should never extend beyond the imaginary line the pencil creates. This will keep your eyes appearing more open and alive. Notice that the arch of the brow is found with the line from the nose up through the iris, and the inside of the brow should align no farther in than the straight line up from the nose to the brow. Lips should be soft and more natural in color, the way you had as a child.

Remember dark colors recede features, and light ones bring forward features. When eyes are a bit more dramatic, lips should stay soft. Lips can be bolder when eyes are more subdued. Again, as we get older the lips thin out, so they need to be more prominent with color. If you are using more dramatic eye colors, as in a smoky-eye look, be careful not to overly do it, and use a softer lip. If you are going for the Audrey Hepburn or Taylor Swift look of simple darker eye liner and natural shadows, you can use a bit more drama on your lips.

Stage make-up with stage lighting can be a bit more dramatic or pronounced so you look natural to the audience. So be careful when you are on camera for TV and video. The camera requires much more subtle make-up. Be more natural in your approach with eyeliner embedded deep at lash base, mascara, soft blush on apples of cheeks, and soft color on lips. Avoid heavy foundation, as the camera picks up details well, and caking foundation looks terrible on camera. If the TV camera is HD, it shows every pore on your face, so extra caution should be used with the subtlety of your make-up.

Now that you are all put together and look great, it is important to inspect your attitude as part of professionalism. Are you ready to speak with great openness and enthusiasm, coming from an authentic heart? Then there is one more thing to consider in your wardrobe and attitude. Clothe yourself with what I call my "Colossians" clothes of compassion, kindness, humility, gentleness, patience, and forgiveness. Then allow yourself to be submerged and surrounded with love and God's peace (Colossians 3:12–14).

Now You Are Ready to Be Anchored and Shine with Brilliance!

Anchor yourself. Stand up in what we call **stature**. Stand and pull your arms straight up in the air over your head as into the ceiling. Pull hard. Now pull straight out to your sides. Drop your arms, but leave your chest up where your pulling allowed it to go. Attach an imaginary bungee cord to the crown of your head where the top of your head starts to turn to go down the back of your head, and feel it pull you into the ceiling. You should feel at least one half inch taller. This also aligns your body in a healthy posture. The ear should now align with your shoulder, waist, hip, knee, and ankle.

Feel the floor come up through your feet, and feel your core going down into the floor, as your bungee pulls you up. This is called grounding yourself. This stature and grounding also keeps you from extraneous distracting movement on stage, or "noodling around," as I call it.

Close your eyes and thank God for who He is and who He has created you to be — very special. Now think of three words that are descriptive of you all the time. No caveats like "only when I feel like…" You are perhaps loving, kind, and creative all the time. Or maybe you are joyful, faithful, and intelligent all the time. Select three words that describe "you," that work for you. Just keep them positive, as if God gave them to you, because, in fact, He did. These are your words and can change as you use your "stature" exercise when speaking.

Take a deep, loving breath and blow it out through pursed lips like blowing out a candle. Allow your body to relax while still in stature, and then take in another deep loving breath and gently blow it out. Relax with each breath.

Now open your eyes and say your name and your three words. "I am (<u>your</u> <u>name),</u> and I am_____, _____, and_____. How do you feel? Do it again with even more enthusiasm.

(*Remember, breath always comes in response to thought. So don't focus on the breath for your name, etc. Just think about saying your name, your three words, and allow your now relaxed breathing pattern to take over.*)

How do you feel?

Do you like and trust yourself?

Are you ready to respect and love your audience?

Are you ready to give your gift of your message to them?

Remember, you really are awesome. I just want **you** to realize it. God knows it and knew it when He made you for this wonderful moment of now, delivering your unique and brilliant message.

Anchor Yourself Further.

Think of a time when you knew you were on top of the world and felt awesome. Really **feel** the emotion of it, like your wedding day or graduation, or a time when you just "nailed" your song or speech. Thank God for it.

After experiencing the strong emotion that makes you tingle physically with the joy and thankfulness of the emotional moment, **anchor** it with a strong physical fist pull with elbows slightly bent and in front of you, ready to be pulled into your body strongly, and say, "Yes!" loudly as you pull! Do it again even stronger!

The reason this works is that your spirit, mind/brain, and body are dramatically connected as you physically anchor a strong, joyful, and thankful emotion. That same strong, joyful, and thankful emotion can be brought back up when the same physical **pull** or **anchor** is used—as in readying yourself to do an amazing speech or song!

Now you are ready to go out there and give your gift.

Chapter 10

THE POWER OF PRESENCE, ENGAGEMENT AND STORY, ON STAGE OR CAMERA

Story: The Woman at the Well

John 4: Jesus realized that the Pharisees were keeping count of the baptisms that he and John performed (although his disciples, not Jesus, did the actual baptizing). They had posted the score that Jesus was ahead, turning him and John into rivals in the eyes of the people. So Jesus left the Judean countryside and went back to Galilee.

To get there, he had to pass through Samaria. He came into Sychar, a Samaritan village that bordered the field Jacob had given his son Joseph. Jacob's well was still there. Jesus, worn out by the trip, sat down at the well. It was noon.

A woman, a Samaritan, came to draw water. Jesus said, "Would you give me a drink of water?" (His disciples had gone to the village to buy food for lunch.)

The Samaritan woman, taken aback, asked, "How come you, a Jew, are asking me, a Samaritan woman, for a drink?" (Jews in those days wouldn't be caught dead talking to Samaritans.)

Jesus answered, "If you knew the generosity of God and who I am, you would be asking me for a drink, and I would give you fresh, living water."

The woman said, "Sir, you don't even have a bucket to draw with, and this well is deep. So how are you going to get this 'living water'? Are you a better man than our ancestor Jacob, who dug this well and drank from it, he and his sons and livestock, and passed it down to us?"

Jesus said, "Everyone who drinks this water will get thirsty again and again. Anyone who drinks the water I give will never thirst—not ever. The water I give will be an artesian spring within, gushing fountains of endless life."

The woman said, "Sir, give me this water so I won't ever get thirsty, won't ever have to come back to this well again!"

He said, "Go call your husband and then come back."

"I have no husband," she said.

"That's nicely put: 'I have no husband.' You've had five husbands, and the man you're living with now isn't even your husband. You spoke the truth there, sure enough."

"Oh, so you're a prophet! Well, tell me this: Our ancestors worshiped God at this mountain, but you Jews insist that Jerusalem is the only place for worship, right?"

"Believe me, woman, the time is coming when you Samaritans will worship the Father neither here at this mountain nor there in Jerusalem. You worship guessing in the dark; we Jews worship in the clear light of day. God's way of salvation is made available through the Jews. But the time is coming—it has, in fact, come—when what you're called will not matter and where you go to worship will not matter.

"It's who you are and the way you live that count before God. Your worship must engage your spirit in the pursuit of truth. That's the kind of people the Father is out looking for: those who are simply and honestly themselves before him in their worship. God is sheer being itself—Spirit. Those who worship him must do it out of their very being, their spirits, their true selves, in adoration."

The woman said, "I don't know about that. I do know that the Messiah is coming. When he arrives, we'll get the whole story."

"I am he," said Jesus. "You don't have to wait any longer or look any further."

Just then his disciples came back. They were shocked. They couldn't believe he was talking with that kind of a woman. No one said what they were all thinking, but their faces showed it.

The woman took the hint and left. In her confusion she left her water pot. Back in the village she told the people, "Come see a man who knew all about the things I did, who knows me inside and out. Do you think this could be the Messiah?" And they went out to see for themselves. —John 4:1–30, **The Message (MSG)**

Story: Parable of the Lost Son

Luke 15:11 Then [Jesus] said, "There was once a man who had two sons. The younger said to his father, 'Father, I want right now what's coming to me.'

"So the father divided the property between them. It wasn't long before the younger son packed his bags and left for a distant country. There, undisciplined and dissipated, he wasted everything he had. After he had gone through all his money, there was a bad famine all through that country and he began to hurt. He signed on with a citizen there who assigned him to his fields to slop the pigs. He was so hungry he would have eaten the corncobs in the pig slop, but no one would give him any.

"That brought him to his senses. He said, 'All those farmhands working for my father sit down to three meals a day, and here I am starving to death. I'm going back to my father. I'll say to him, Father, I've sinned against God, I've sinned before you; I don't deserve to be called your son. Take me on as a hired hand.' He got right up and went home to his father.

"When he was still a long way off, his father saw him. His heart pounding, he ran out, embraced

him, and kissed him. The son started his speech: 'Father, I've sinned against God, I've sinned before you; I don't deserve to be called your son ever again.'

"But the father wasn't listening. He was calling to the servants, 'Quick. Bring a clean set of clothes and dress him. Put the family ring on his finger and sandals on his feet. Then get a grain-fed heifer and roast it. We're going to feast! We're going to have a wonderful time! My son is here — given up for dead and now alive! Given up for lost and now found!' And they began to have a wonderful time.

"All this time his older son was out in the field. When the day's work was done he came in. As he approached the house, he heard the music and dancing. Calling over one of the houseboys, he asked what was going on. He told him, 'Your brother came home. Your father has ordered a feast — barbecued beef! — because he has him home safe and sound.'

"The older brother stalked off in an angry sulk and refused to join in. His father came out and tried to talk to him, but he wouldn't listen. The son said, 'Look how many years I've stayed here serving you, never giving you one moment of grief, but have you ever thrown a party for me and my *friends? Then this son of yours who has thrown away your money on whores shows up and you go all out with a feast!'*

"His father said, 'Son, you don't understand. You're with me all the time, and everything that is mine is yours—but this is a wonderful time, and we have to celebrate. This brother of yours was dead, and he's alive! He was lost, and he's found!'"—Luke 15:11–32, The Message (MSG)

Vocal Application: *These stories are powerful for several reasons. The first shows how Jesus engaged this woman and used His presence and special knowlege about her to continue to engage her by asking her questions, even though the cultural norm was that He should not be talking to her. Stories are very powerful because they are engaging, and when the teller uses the power of presence, engaging questions, and interest creating techniques, they are a most effective way of communicating a message or point of a message. The result of the interaction in this story led her to believe and tell everyone about Jesus. Notice she went from calling Him "Jew," to "Sir," to finally calling him "Prophet," knowing all she did, and finally, "Messiah."*

The power of your presence is important in communicating and having an impactful influence. There are five elements of presence that must be paid attention to because they are keys in your speaking. Jesus was very engaging and told great stories, some called parables, where He captivated and made others think deeply with analagous stories to make His strong points.

The story of the lost son was told for people to relate to and see the strong and unconditional love of God has toward us. It also shows the strong human tendency toward jealousy and unforgiveness, but also the celebratory nature of God's forgiveness.

There is great power in storytelling. Develope your own story in an effective way with powerful presence and engagement so the audience will truly lean in and want more of you and what you have to offer.

I want to begin this chapter by giving you a clearer understanding of presence, as it is associated with elements of our God-given planet earth. These elements and associated meanings, virtues, and delivery keys are helpful in better understanding presence as a total concept.

Presence associated with the element of METAL — Acknowledge Others, Be Clear: Virtue is Courage; Delivery Keys are Authenticity and Clarity (No B.S., Get to the Point)

What does it mean to be clear? As the element of metal suggests, be clear. Be authentic, and get to the point. Don't use extraneous or "out there" concepts, no exaggeration, or rabbit trailing off your subject. Be concrete versus ethereal. Acknowledge others with clarity and authenticity.

An important part of your ability to connect with your audience is your ability to be absolutely CLEAR with your message, your intent, your body, and voice. Clarity of message, purpose, and intent is critical. So as you put your message together, be aware of these things. It takes **courage** to be disciplined and clear. It is an important observation that being real and even emotional at times denotes authenticity. When you are sad and feel like crying, you are very real to others. Always allow yourself to be courageously real. That does not mean emotionally loosing control of yourself, but being vulnerable is being real and can speak in a powerful way that connects to your audience.

You must know WHY you are saying or doing anything in your message. Knowing why you are giving your message helps WHAT you are saying be clear to your audience. HOW you say and deliver your message is also critical to clarity.

Being clear with an open voice (double horn system as discussed in chapter 8), open nonthreatening body posture, and eye contact with each person in your audience are a huge part of your ability to be clear and to connect with your audience. As mentioned before, only seven percent of your communication are your words.

But they are a very important seven percent. The other ninety-three percent are your thought energy, vocal tone, and body language. So while **what** you say is important, **how** you say it us even more important.

Your body should be tall (as in stature), aligned straight, chest up with your shoulders hanging under your ears; but relaxed with feet under hips and long toes forward so your feet are straight and neutral. You do not want your feet angled out, because this subtly says, "cocky," or "arrogant," and pushes your audience away versus drawing them forward to connect with you.

Hands should be neutral and relaxed by your side, at your waist or resting comfortably on your note stand, never gripping it, as in a death grip! Hands only come up with genuine expression congruent with what you are saying. As to camera work, hands need to be comfortably at your waist or bustline, in the frame and moving to emphasize your points. You don't want them to be bobbing in and out of the frame. More on camera later in the chapter.

Some people pace to one side of the room and then the other in an effort to connect with everyone in the room. If your message indicates a move, then move. But keep movement meaningful to your message. Remember, any motion of your body must be congruent and have meaning with your message, or it becomes a distraction away from your message. Pacing is a huge distraction. Address everyone in your audience, but with purpose and intention from where you are with **some** meaningful movement versus movement for movement sake.

Presence associated with the element of FIRE—Connection, Ignite: Virtue is Joy; Delivery Keys are Connection, Passion, Joy, Humor, and Energy

The next element is fire or connection. **Ignite** your audience with passion, joy, humor, and energy. Use your heart connection and your real passion to **ignite** your message. This connects or creates relationship with those in your audience.

We all have a sense of humor, even if you think you are not a "funny" person. It is important to realize, as the Bible tells us, that laughter is healing to your body and bones—as well as the bodies and bones of others.

Doing improvisation is a great way to build confidence in your ability to use humor in your messages and situations as you are dealing with anything that an audience can experience with you during a speech. I find that people who think they are not funny become very clever and quite funny during improvisational exercises.

A great improvisational exercise is as follows:

In a one-minute time frame, you are given a theme for a story. You begin to create and speak your story. Then you are given a new word to be incorporated in the story a few seconds into your story. You are given a new word every few seconds to incorporate. You will be amazed how funny this story becomes. You begin to relax into your humor and enjoy your funny bone! I have watched people who are very serious and think they are not funny become extremely funny as they trust their instincts and go for it.

God has given us all a sense of humor, and using it actually makes you feel good and able to trust yourself in any situation.

Relax and let God show you the humor in any situation. Dislike and sadness are the other side of the coin of joy. Humor comes out of real life, and dislike and sadness become joy and laughter when you can see the reality and ridiculousness of dislike, hate, or even sadness in a situation. Connection is our goal with this element, so ignite your audience and see your connection become even stronger.

Presence associated with the element of EARTH—Serve Others, Ground: Virtue is Fairness; Delivery Keys are Body, Groundedness, Practical, Simplicity

The next element of presence is earth or grounding. To be grounded means to **serve others** by founding, establishing, educating, tutoring, or training. Your ability to be grounded is to be fair, practical, and simplistic. Interestingly, taste is the sense that is associated here. You can establish a connection to being relaxed and grounded with a sip of water, or a grape in your mouth. When used in a grounded and relaxed confident state, these become triggers to help you stay grounded when you feel your body and mind start to become ungrounded or anxious.

Singing is another very grounding activity. I always get my speakers singing because it builds their confidence and understanding of their voices and bodies. Singing and speaking require full body incorporation.

Grounding is important because it gives you authority to teach, coach, tutor, or serve others better. A posture that really grounds you is called **stature**. Standing in stature as discussed in chapters 8 and 9 by stretching your arms up over head into the ceiling, then stretching them out horizontally with the floor, allows you to leave your chest up while relaxing your shoulders as you lower your arms to your side. Now your body is tall and straight, and your head is held up from an imaginary bungee cord coming out the crown of your head. It is a bungee, so you can move comfortably. This is the first piece of grounding. Next, you would feel the floor coming up through your straight feet, which are neutrally under your hips with long toes pointing forward. Then your body core must go down into the floor between your feet as you remain tall and strong, head up and shoulders hanging from their pivot point of the center where the two clavicle or collarbones come together.

You will now feel grounded into the space you occupy. This allows you to be connected confidently with your body, message, and audience. You are now strong, but relaxed and very confident with the gift of you and your message that you are delivering.

Being physically grounded moves your mind to feel grounded as well. The spirit, mind/brain, and body connection is so strong that when your body is strong, your mind wants to assume the same strength, and then your spirit kicks in to center you in your groundedness. It is a powerful connection and truly grounds you. Your audience, no matter how large or small, will sense your grounding and want to lean in and take all the good you came to give.

Presence associated with the element of WATER—Be Curious, Go with the Flow: Virtues are Less Fear/More Gentleness; Delivery Keys are Vulnerability, Softness, Receptivity, Compassion, Flexibility and Fluidity

This next element is all about being curious and going with the flow of what is happening around you. Go with less fear and more gentleness. Be vulnerable, soft, receptive, compassionate, and flexible. Listening with your two ears as you speak with your one mouth helps you be more present to others and God. Listening helps you go with the flow of anything that comes your way.

There is a term called "what is-ing," meaning go with what is. Say you are speaking and a phone goes off. Do you ignore it? No, you acknowledge it and perhaps use humor to incorporate the obvious into your message. If you have set parameters as to phone use and consequences before your speech, this gives you a great opportunity to have fun with a consequence action using loving humor. This acknowledgment becomes an engagement technique that puts your audience at ease and re-engages them with you and your message.

Another example could be a backdrop falls, or a huge loud noise from outside invades your space and message. How would you handle this? You might make up a cute story as to what it was or why it happened. The main thing is to **acknowledge** and continue with everyone re-engaged with you and your message. Because you dealt with the obvious, the audience respects and engages more with you. The distraction becomes minimal, and you can carry on with your presentation.

It helps you to stay confidently in control when you know you can handle anything that could happen while speaking. Remember to always acknowledge whatever it may be that is a distraction or interruption and "go with the flow." Make it work for you. Your audience will love you and respect you for it. Your compassion and flexibility are great connectors and increase your presence greatly.

Presence associated with the element of WOOD—Give Choice, Direct the Flow: Virtue is Kindness; Delivery Keys are Boldness, Power, Command, Confidence

The final element is wood and directing the flow with confident power. Give choice to people. While shouting can be the sound associated here, I prefer you to think of projection (opening your vocal horns and speaking appropriately to fill the room with your voice). Anger and kindness are a two-sided coin. Rather than sounding angry, you want to be open and project kindness. Delivery keys here are boldness, power, command, and confidence. Seeing and observing your audience is crucial so you can keep a reading on the energy and feelings of your audience. You must look people in the eyes and scan the room to see everyone so they know you have seen them as you speak.

I like to emphasize another P word, passion with powerful directing. As you tap into your genuine passion for your subject and message content, your bold power comes through that passion. It is infectious and very influential.

How you think is critical to the success of speaking. Every thought you have is connected to emotion and creates an electrical chemical energy field that emanates from you. Others pick up on what you think, so you are communicating without saying a word. When you are connected to your passion and power, your thoughts are all about your audience and not yourself. That passion and connection are where the **power** is. When your words are one thing, but your thoughts are another (such as "will they like me" or other self-conscious thoughts), the message that is loudest to your audience is what your thoughts are saying. Your thoughts must be congruent with your message or gift to your audience. Once you tap into your love for giving your gift to the audience and your total presentation is about **them** and **not you**, you will get hooked on the awesome feeling of speaking your gift. Directing with appropriate loving power and boldness is a natural by-product.

Your total presence (all five elements) on stage and off must be the same. There is no such thing as "stage presence" apart from the real you and how you are with people all the time. If you are timid with people or wild and crazy, your presence needs to be more balanced and improved. By being **connected and clear, funny, grounded, fluid and relaxed, and passionately strong and powerful,** you will be your most effective with people whether on stage or not. Even a one-on-one meeting with someone demonstrates your understanding of true presence by being clear, connected, grounded, fluid, humorous, and strong. You should always be the same on and off stage, **full of great presence**.

"Tell me and I forget. Teach me and I remember. Involve me and I learn."

This is a true statement. The power of engagement, or involving your audience with you, is a critical piece to effective learning. The brain needs to be re-engaged every five to seven minutes. That means a good speaker uses tools to keep the audience involved and engaged every five to seven minutes during their speech. Some of these are physical and some mental. Some good physical tools are as follows: having the audience Hi-five with a person next to them, or share with that person a statement that pertains to what you just said in your message, affirming the point of your message just made. Have them lean forward and unlock an imaginary combination lock of what you want them to remember, such as 24-7-10 to represent learning being locked in if you revisit the information within twenty-four hours, in seven days, and again in ten days on-going.

Mental ones can be asking a question, such as, "Would you not agree that... (statement you want to share in an engaging way)?" Another mental tool is having your audience fill in the blank of a statement you make, then pausing so that the audience can complete the sentence in their own words.

Talking heads do not truly teach without a learning or involvement strategy so that your audience is moving physically and mentally in engagement. Your presence and ability to share your story and stories in your message will teach in a powerful way that will allow people to learn effectively.

Receiving coaching in these elements of presence and engagement in a manner where you are involved is critical for you to learn them. Again, I am here to serve you. My contact information is at the back of this book. Call me or email me so you may experience coaching with me as your mentor and friend.

Your story and how to put it together to engage your audience, is the last piece of this chapter. I am going to borrow a term and some teaching from one of my favorite trainers, Callan Rush.[4] That term is a Turning Point Story.

What Is a Turning Point Story?

A Turning Point Story is a strategic, personal life story shared by you, designed to quickly demonstrate your specific expertise while expressing your general humanity.

An effective Turning Point Story sets the context for your time on stage. When designed and delivered well, it positions your specific audience psychologically in a way that optimizes their ability to receive the message and information you want to give them.

What makes you a successful speaker or singer? The success of your speaking stems from your ability to create trusting intimate relationships with your audience. When your audience feels they are in a trusting intimate relationship with you, assuming you are solving their specialized problems, they will happily listen to you, attend your events, and purchase products and programs from you on an ongoing basis if your business has them.

Your top priority, then, must be to create powerful, trusting, intimate relationships as quickly and effectively as possible. This is where a solid Turning Point Story can help.

The foundation of all powerful, trusting, intimate relationships is communication, and the best communicators in the world are "Charismatic Communicators."

Charisma is that rare, attractive, and charming personal quality attributed to leaders who inspire devotion and enthusiasm. Charisma creates personal magnetism and enables you to greatly influence others. Your Turning Point Story will help you reveal your natural charisma, thereby increasing your ability to influence.

Mind you, every one of you can have charisma regardless of your personality. So, no excuses here! God created you with gifting inside and charisma that is natural to you.

Your charisma, as experienced by others, is directly proportional to your ability to demonstrate your **expertise** and your **humanity.**

Expertise refers to your ability to demonstrate you are a competent professional or an expert in your field.

Humanity refers to your ability to demonstrate you are a human being just like the members of your audience, who face the same problems, pains, and dilemmas.

Demonstrating equal amounts of expertise and humanity allows your audience to like, trust, and respect you instantly. When this happens, not only will they be willing to believe what you say, but they'll also be willing to buy what you sell.

Most speakers who are workshop, seminar, and church leaders, or who are business owners, or in business as entrepreneurs do a good job of demonstrating one or the other (expertise OR humanity)—but most don't understand how to balance the two.

If you demonstrate too much expertise, you may risk your audience feeling like you are indeed an expert in your field—but that they could never achieve what you have. They'll think you've had special training, experience, or mentorship that they haven't. The result? They won't buy from you because they won't think they can do what you do or did. If they do buy from you, they'll often second-guess and cancel shortly thereafter. I know this can be an issue in network marketing. That is why duplicatable processes are so important.

If you demonstrate too much humanity, your audience will undoubtedly love you. They will relate to you, and feel you are just like them. Unfortunately, they won't buy from you because they won't feel like you have the necessary expertise to take them where they want to go.

An effective Turning Point Story (whether used live, in print, on camera or on line) helps you demonstrate BOTH your expertise and your humanity in a balanced way. It's the best and quickest way to reveal your natural charisma and have your audience eating out of the palm of your hand!

In other words, when you express your Turning Point Story well, your audience will be inspired to connect and bond with you at a deep level, while heightening their respect for you as an expert. Overall, they will be much more open to receiving the gifts you want to offer them.

A Turning Point Story is a relevant, **intentionally crafted story** taken from some period of your life. The story details a time in your life when you reached a new level of understanding and realization after experiencing some type of challenge and adversity.

Imbedded in the story will be a Turning Point, the exact moment of realization or awakening that shifted your life and gave you a new, more empowered perspective. It is the point at which you gained the key insight or information that allowed you to rise up and improve or enhance the overall quality of your life. Personal testimony stories of how life was before believing in Jesus, then finding and accepting Christ's gift of salvation and all the amazing benefits of that decision in your life now are great Turning Point Stories in ministry.

Your Turning Point Story does not need to detail a big, dramatic event. It can do that, or it can be one of many smaller turning points in your life. The key is to make sure the story is relevant to your audience, has particular significance and meaning to you, and is also relevant to the message you are about to share.

Please keep in mind you are storytelling. You are not manipulating, but crafting and expressing your personal story in a way that invokes the imagination of your audience. Well-told stories can be very engaging and effective.

A Turning Point Story is not a strict statement of details and facts. It is about creativity. You can tweak timelines and events to weave a masterful image. You must paint meaningful word pictures with your stories. Jesus did this very well in His parables, or allegorical stories.

Your Turning Point Story is really about involving your audience so they can enter in and participate in your life with you. Like any great story, you want to take your audience on a journey complete with trials, tribulations, and triumphs. You are literally taking them on an emotional roller-coaster ride while making absolute certain you are demonstrating your expertise and your humanity along the way.

Where Can You Use Your Turning Point Story?

There are many places in your speaking or singing where you'll want to demonstrate your charisma, which will make your potential clients like, trust, and respect you immediately. You can use full or modified versions of your Turning Point Story at each of these places. Here are some examples:

- At the beginning of any live speaking engagement, workshop or seminar
- In your professional bio

- On your website under, "About Us"
- At networking events and gatherings where you have a very short time to speak
- On teleclasses, interviews, and webinars
- With a friend who wants to hear your story of experience with Jesus, but has never met Him yet

In summary, your Turning Point Story is one of the most leveraged and powerful ways to establish an instant intimate relationship with your audience. You will craft different versions of the same Turning Point Story, or craft entirely new Turning Point Stories depending on whom you are speaking to, and what your topic is.[4]

You are building a bridge of communication, not burning the bridge. Remember this when sharing your story or stories of Jesus in your real life. Keep your language real and understandable for your listener—no Christian-eese (faith terms they won't understand). Use tact, diplomacy, and sensitivity to them when telling your story. Make a point without making an enemy.

The power of your presence, engagement techniques, and charismatic stories are all part of a masterful and honest connection with your audience, whether it be one or many. Use them well.

Camera Technique Tips

You may have a professional videographer, but most people do not, because they prefer to shoot their own videos. When videoing yourself, there are things you want to be aware of that make big differences in your effectiveness on screen and in your overall impact. If you choose to use your smart phone, iPhone, iPad, or tablet, be sure it is stable on a stand or tripod. Turn the camera or phone so that the frame is horizontal (wider and short in height), instead of vertical (tall and narrow). This allows you to look taller and in control.

Also, you want your head at the top of the frame, with a close-up shot with your hands comfortable at bust height. This may feel strange, but it looks great on camera. This positioning of comfortable hands higher than normal keeps your hands in the frame so that movement is natural and stays in the frame. You do not want your hands coming in and out of the frame. This is very distracting. And if your hands are moving too far forward, they can look gigantic and out of proportion. Keep them touching at your center — bust height.

Callan Rush

While I cannot read what the words say in this head shot of the little girl, the position of the hands and body denoting emotion are great. Notice the background is stark white, or simple gray, with a bit of texture and text over the top. These work well. Some people use a green screen, or invisible background, where any image can be inserted, as used on news weather casts.

Another point is to keep your clothing neat and simple. Make sure not to use "gaudy" jewelry as well so as to not be distracting. Prints, stripes, and multicolored clothing can be very distracting on camera. Keep it simple with solid colors.

Be sure there is great lighting. If you don't have access to great lighting, then shoot your video outside on an overcast day. This makes for good light on your face without a need to squint. Light on your face is important and can make you look young and vibrant as well. Look out for shadows on your face or distractions in the frame. They can sabotage your energetic look on camera, and can create distraction (a tree blowing back and forth in the wind, or wind blowing your hair in your face, etc.)

Make sure there is good audio. Be sure you are using a lapel microphone plugged to your camera if possible. If not, be sure you are close enough to good audio in your tablet or phone microphone. Test it out and be sure you have a good sound source.

It is important that your background be simple as well. Cluttered areas behind you are distracting and take focus away from you. A simple solid wall (no shadows), or a simple room with only a book or two, or one picture behind you, can work to add warmth, which will not distract your audience away from you and your message.

Stand up to shoot video because it helps your energy and helps you to focus on your audience and message. Remember, you are only speaking to **one** good friend on the other side of the camera. That is important in order to create the intimacy you must have with your audience of **one.**

I have found that if I turn the camera to a "selfie" position on the tripod or stand, so I can see myself delivering to my **one** great friend, it helps me deliver better because I can relax yet monitor how I am coming across to myself as I speak.

Lastly, be sure you have a pleasant look on your face. Smile and enjoy!

Chapter 11

WHAT DOES PERSONALITY HAVE TO DO WITH IT?

"If it is possible, as far as it depends on you, be at peace with all people." —**Romans 12:18,** (NIV)

Vocal Application: *All personalities are unique and different from others. We are all gifted and unique, so we must understand ourselves as well as others in order to be effective as speakers and, as such, communicators. Being at peace with yourself allows you to be at peace with others by being willing to understand your needs and the needs of others, thus giving them what they need to receive from you based on their emotional psychological needs, not yours.*

Why Don't You Think Like Me?[5]

W hat does personality understanding have to do with voice? Knowing who you are is vital to your ability to communicate with other people. Your voice is intimately connected to your uniqueness. Just as chapters 1-3 discussed the importance of you knowing who you are, this chapter defines you more specifically as to your personality, and all the life influencers to your unique personality.

God's gift to you is your unique personality. Your gift back to God is what you do with who you are. Understanding yourself and what your unique emotional and psychological needs are, so you can be effective in accepting yourself and communicating with the people in your life, brings glory to God. Not only is it important to understand yourself, you must also understand others in your life, who they are, what their personality is, and their unique needs. God calls us to love others as we love ourselves. How can you love others as yourself if you don't understand, accept, and love yourself, and understand or "get" who they really are?

Your credibility is at stake with others in your understanding how to be an effective communicator, including knowing the personality and emotional needs of the other person.

So What Do You Do with the Difficult Person in Your Life? Read On!

Have you ever considered that you and your life create a beautiful unique melody? And have you considered that the people in your life add the harmony to your life melody, and that together you make music?

As stated before, I am a long-time musician, voice teacher, professional singer, and trainer. As such, I love to use music as an analogy to aid learning. When examining and listening to music, you will find a wide variance in harmonies. Some harmonies are dissonant, and create tension, while others are pleasant and soothing, or harmonious, as we say. But whether dissonant or harmonious, they still create music when combined with melody.

Relationships are the same. Have you experienced people in your life who simply create tension and stress? They are dissonant with you, while some relationships are always pleasant, soothing, and harmonious with you. Why is that?

People are different. I know that sounds too obvious, but those differences cause all the problems and challenges, while others create all the joy and good feelings in your life. You and I must celebrate the differences by identifying, understanding, and giving the unique other person what they need.

You are born with a part of your personality that was an established part of you when you were conceived. It remains a huge part of you consistently until you leave this earth. Then there are five other life influencers that contribute to your over-all personality. Everyone sees the world through colored glasses or lenses. Mine may be pink, while yours may be blue. I see the world warm and rosy, while you see it cool and blue. We may be a bit dissonant at times, or difficult. Or we may make great **purple** harmony together, as blue and pink mix well to create purple. People often are attracted to opposite personalities. They love each other and make lovely music together, but can drive each other crazy at times and be very dissonant or difficult.

You exhibit preferences that are evident in the personally unique ways in how you react to your surroundings, and those preferences are reflected in your different needs, wants, and values. You perceive based on your personal preference filter, or the "lenses you wear." Then your perception causes you to approach the situation in a certain way. Based on your perception and approach, you will interact with the situation a certain way unique to you. If people perceive differently, they will approach differently, and certainly interact with people and the environment differently.

God made each of us unique. In Psalms 139, it says God created your inmost being, He knit you together in your mother's womb, and that you were fearfully and wonderfully made. It also says that all your days were written in His book before one of them came to be.

> *"Before I (God) formed you in the womb I knew you, and before you were born I set you apart. I appointed you as a prophet to the nations." —* Jeremiah 1:5, (NIV)

The trick to making beautiful music in relationships is to understand and celebrate those God-given differences in people's unique personalities, then adapt to their needs, wants, and values versus forcing ours on them. Bible Scripture tells us:

> *"If it is possible, as far as it depends on you, live at peace with everyone"* —Romans 12:18, (NIV)

How can you possibly be at peace with others if you don't have a clue as to who they are or how they perceive, approach life, or interact with it and you; or what they need, want, and value?

> Scripture also says, *"Do not let any unwholesome talk come out of your mouths, but only what is helpful for building others up according to their needs, that it may benefit those who listen, or be a blessing to the hearer."* —Ephesians 4:29, (NIV)

How can you be a blessing to the other person if you don't know what will bless them? We usually keep trying to give them what **we** want them to hear versus what they need to hear, want to hear, and value hearing.

There are and have been many personality systems over the years to help you discover your psychological personality. It all began with Hippocrates' scientific work as a Greek physician in four hundred BC. But I have discovered in my four decades of studying and searching out effective information for helping people understand and deal healthily and easily with themselves and others that you need a good understanding of your in-born personality and all the major influencers to be able to bring out the best in yourself and others. The best I have experienced are the tools and leadership of CRGleader of Canada and Dr. Ken Keis.[5]

> ***Personal Style is your natural predisposition to perceive, approach, and interact with the environment in a preferred way— Your natural predisposition towards time, tasks, people and situations.[5]***

Including your in-born personality, or **Personal Style** as defined in the tools from Consulting Resource Group in Canada, there are six factors to personality and differences. There are three internal and there are three external influencers.

The internal ones are:[5]

1. Biophysical influences (genetics, sickness, birth defects, allergies, gender, body type, addictions, bodily malfunctions, stress-related illness, biochemical imbalances, health and wellness issues, physical and mental challenges)

2. In-born psychological personality, **Personal Style** (the part of you that you are born with and that does not change over time. It is not learned, but is natural to you.)

3. Self-worth levels (overall value you place on your total being—the measurement of the deepest level of relationship you have with yourself. Other than your relationship with God, the most important relationship you will have, and the one you will see all the others by, is your relationship with yourself.)

The external personality factors are:[5]

4. Traumatic experiences (divorce, physical attack, verbal abuse, sexual assault, road accidents, failed investments, house fires, intimidation, war experiences, natural catastrophes, job termination, death of a loved one, ill health, losing a limb, being rejected in love, seeing someone killed, public embarrassment, attempting suicide, etc.)

5. Social teachers (parents, brothers, sisters, grandparents, aunts, uncles, cousins, in-laws, school teachers, coaches, friends, peers, neighbors, religious leaders, girlfriends, boyfriends, spouses, actors, rock stars, supervisors, authors, artists, etc.)

6. Environmental systems (the experiential stimulus we receive from our environment that comes from being members of certain social and cultural groups—family of origin, step-families, foster families, organizations, communities, religious groups, cultures, school systems, places of work, geographic settings, climatic conditions, natural catastrophes, cult groups, military service, etc.)

So there is an unchangeable part of you (your in-born **Personal Style**), and there are changeable parts of your personality (the other five elements). These two seemingly contradictory phenomena allow your personality to have flexibility and stability throughout life. This means you can seem to change over time and yet still be the same. An example would be meeting someone at your school reunion; at first you don't recognize them, but as you talk with them, you start to recognize the person who was there when in school, the one they have always been.

It is important to note that all attitudes and behaviors are socially learned and reinforced; therefore, all the behaviors, attitudes, and beliefs you have can be **relearned** if you are not satisfied with them, or they are not serving you healthily and well.

Let's look at the relationships that seem to be the most important to the majority of people, and how best to communicate in those relationships. What do you do when the person you thought was so perfect, who you devoted your life to and married, seems to be so wrong for you now at this moment?

What do you do when those sweet little babies turn out to be so different from you and your husband, and they are driving you crazy?

What do you do when you find yourself working with associates or bosses who appear to be from another planet and communication has gone all wrong or is nonexistent?

First of all, you must come to really know and understand the great, unique, and awesome person you are. God doesn't make mistakes, and He created you with specific combinations of personality traits. The reason it is so vital to know yourself is that you will see and relate to everyone through your special filters. Knowing what those filters are helps you accept who you are, so you can learn to love and celebrate yourself in a new way, making it ultimately easier to understand another person.

> Jesus tells us: *"For the entire law is fulfilled in keeping this one command: 'Love your neighbor as yourself.'"*—Galatians 5:14, (NIV).

How can you possibly love others as yourself if you've never come to know, understand, and deeply love yourself?

Just as music is created by specific melodies (you) and harmonies (others), music also has specific styles. You can have the same music played in the style of jazz, pop, gospel, rock, country, or classical. The difference is the arrangement of the notes in the music to create different-sounding melodies, harmonies, and rhythms. The same holds true for the different personality styles in people, thus affecting relationships. Everyone has an in-born personality pattern. Personality patterns can be described best by using four basic dimensions, which correspond to the four primary areas of human interaction: (Popular) Affective, (Powerful) Behavioral, (Perfect) Cognitive, and (Peaceful) Interpersonal, (As described in Personal Style indicator from CRGleader, Canada. The descriptive words in parentheses are mine). No personality consists of just one dimension, but a combination of all four.

Like different pieces of music composed of the same notes, but different arrangement of those notes, we are different compositions of the same personality dimensions. And as the arrangement and duration of notes in a piece of music create a certain style of music, the various intensities (or degrees) of Personal Style dimensions in an individual create a certain Personal Style pattern.

Like dancing to different beats in music, people have deeply engrained motivations for why they prefer to dance to one beat versus another in life choices and interactions. Let's look at the four areas of in-born personality as follows:

Popular Affective—the need to **Influence**

Powerful Behavioral—the natural orientation toward **Action**

Perfect Cognitive—the tendency to be **Analytical**

Peaceful Interpersonal—the desire for **Harmony**

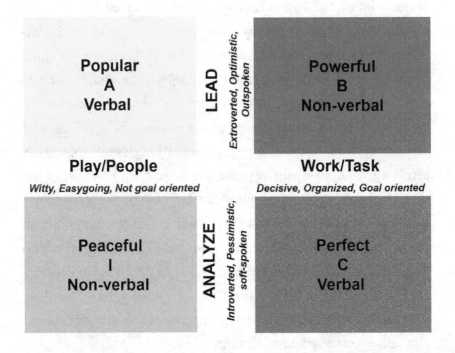

Popular Andy or Anna Affective: He and she are highly creative thinkers and are very expressive. They exhibit creative energy and therefore are the most social and expressive of the four styles. He and she can talk to anyone, anytime, anywhere. While they are very accepting of others, they want their creative ideas to influence them. They will move away quickly from any negativity toward their creative endeavors. They are eternal optimists and dreamers, and require positive energy from those around them. When people or situations restrain the fulfillment of their need to be free from routine, they will bring their power to influence to bear on the problem or situation, attempting to sway people's thoughts and feelings, or they will change their environment.[5]

Popular "A" people love to speak, but they need to listen more, talk less, and be to the point and clear when speaking publicly. They must choose to craft their message carefully and not be quite as "off the cuff" in their delivery. While humor can come very naturally, they need to learn to be more directive and grounded. (See the five elements of presence in chapter 10.)

Powerful Bill or Bonnie Behavioral: He or she is typical of people who score very high in the Personal Style Indicator in the behavioral dimension. They like to set goals, to accomplish pre-determined plans, and to be in control of what is going on around them. They frequently make quick decisions, take on larger responsibilities, and focus on future developments. They prefer strategic thinking, working alone, and being independent. They have a lot of physical energy, are action oriented, and prefer jobs that require risk taking.[5]

Powerful "B" people must be sensitive to their audience and more flexible, relaxed, and have fun when speaking publicly. Realize that others have good opinions also and don't want to be pushed! Lighten up, listen to others, use humor more, and be aware of the audience's need for engagement and positive energy. (See the five elements of presence in chapter 10.)

Perfect Connie or Chris Cognitive: She and he prefer analytical thinking, as mental energy is a key characteristic. They prefer to think rather than do, and tend to constantly question and judge what is going on around them. They evaluate their environment and people in that environment critically, often appearing outspoken, critical, and fast to give advice. They are organized and systematic, and prefer to interact with one person at a time versus many. She and he are very verbal, but only when they are comfortable in their environment. They also quite often show verbal preferences in writing. They perceive well and think deeply about things.[5]

Perfect "C" people must understand that not all of their audience want details, charts, and graphs. Lighten up, use key words, color, pictures and add more fun when speaking publicly. Learn to "go with the flow" more. Spontaneity and humor can be your best friend. Your comfort zone is in your head and can be managed to match your situation in positive light. (See the five elements of presence in chapter 10.)

Peaceful Isabella or Ira Interpersonal: These two are practical thinkers and prefer social harmony. They care about others and work consistently and reliably with them. They are great team players, and love to serve others. Since emotional energy is high, they are sensitive to what others think and say—sometimes overly so. They tend to put others first over themselves even when it may cause discomfort for them. They are nonassertive and have difficulty expressing their feelings and opinions in conflict situations. Even though they love serving others, they do not want the focus on them. They tend to be shy in groups unless they can serve without being in the spotlight.[5]

Peaceful "I" people must be willing to speak up and be heard. If you are a Peaceful "I", know you have something important to say and be willing to step up and say it publicly. Remember

you are awesome and you are a gift to others. All the elements of presence in chapter 10 will serve you well with clarity, humor, groundedness, knowing it is okay to "go with the flow," and directed power and passion.

When speaking to any audience, remember there will be all four personalities in the room. Make it fun for the Popular A, clear and concise for the Powerful B, reliable and factual for the Perfect C, and easy and relaxed for the Peaceful I.

I hope you are beginning to identify yourself, your mate, child, or associate at work or church. In doing so, you are on your way to being able to communicate better with them, but there is more you need to know.

To reiterate, everyone is a combination of these four personality dimensions, but generally you will show up in one or two areas predominantly, thereby being easier to identify by others who desire to communicate well with you.

There are unique combinations of in-born personality, or **Personal Style**, that make you special. They are not difficult to identify, but you need help in knowing how to do that. Knowing what the predominant personality or personalities of someone else and the associated needs are critical to your having credibility and compatibility with that other person.

Also, there is a strong tendency to be attracted to an opposite personality or blend. Peaceful **I** people are attracted to Powerful **B** people, and visa-versa, because the powerful **B** needs peace in their life, and the peaceful **I** enjoys the powerful **B** to take charge in life. Perfect **C** people attract to popular **A's** charm and beauty, while the popular **A** is attracted to the order in the perfect **C**. It also helps to share a personality dimension. For instance, I am a popular **A** and powerful **B**, while my husband is a perfect **C** and powerful **B**. We were attracted as opposites, but share the powerful **B**. We both have been high-impact people, who are great at getting the job done together. The study of personalities, and **Personal Style** in particular, has saved our marriage, as my popular **A** needs and his perfect **C** needs were conflicting. But by understanding each other's unique needs and being willing to meet those needs, we are much more loving and understanding with each other.

Remember:

Popular "A" people emotionally need: attention, affection, approval, acceptance, variety, and play or pleasure.

Powerful "B" people emotionally need: challenge, independence, power, control, responsibility, credit, and appreciation for work.

Perfect "C" people emotionally need: intimacy, organization, respect, safety, space, support, and silence.

Peaceful "I" people emotionally need: harmony, security, loving others, feelings of worth, lack of stress, honor, and peace.

You are familiar, I hope, with the "Golden Rule," which says:

> *"So in everything, do unto others what you would have them do to you, for this sums up the Law of the Prophets."* —Matthew 7:12, (NIV)

On the other hand, the **"Platinum Rule"** is **"Do unto others as they <u>want</u> and <u>need</u> to be done to"**![5]

Each personality responds best to certain approaches. This is important when you are talking to someone or speaking to an audience because there will be some of **all** these personalities in any audience.

Popular "A" people respond best to: admiration for their achievements, unstructured environments, affection, communication, and opportunities to creatively influence.

Powerful "B" people respond best to: summarized facts, direct honest confrontation, support for their goals, and people who are efficient and effective in getting results.

Perfect "C" people respond best to: detailed information, respect for their opinion, systematic and proven approaches, and tasks done well and completely.

Peaceful "I" people respond best to: appreciation for their efforts, non-threatening approaches, thoughtfulness for others, honesty, and trust.

A good technique is to "mirror" the person in front of you at any given time. By that I mean mirror their energy, speaking, timing, etc. This will help you approach them more appropriately.

Jesus Is in the Center of the Personality Chart.

You have strengths and weaknesses, as do all humans. Even your strengths taken to an extreme can become weaknesses. The best news is that Christ represents the strengths of all four personality categories and the weaknesses of none. So as you seek to grow and understand all four of the in-born personalities (Personal Styles), their strengths, weaknesses, and needs, you grow closer to becoming more like Christ.

As you seek to grow closer to Him and obey His ways, you become more balanced and a better communicator. Seek to understand and love yourself and know your needs. Focus on the positives and strengths in yourself and in others. Forgive the negatives and weaknesses in yourself and others, and deliver to them what they need from you

Set Your Style Needs Aside and Focus on the Person or Audience in Front of You.

Celebrate the differences as you seek to be a better communicator through your voice. Tonality reflects emotion and comes through the voice loud and clear. You cannot hide your thoughts and emotions that are tied to those thoughts. Remember, thoughts are electrical-chemical and send out an energy field that speaks louder than your words. So be aware of yourself, what you are thinking and feeling as you speak, so you can truly be effective in speaking or singing to an audience. If you are fearful, or silly, or stern, or boring in your approach, people will read you like a book, and your words will not be heard or appreciated well. Remember the seven percent rule that states that only seven percent of your communication are words. The ninety-three percent communicates through your voice, expression, and body language, or your whole personality.

This information will improve your marriages by understanding the truth of love and respect and celebrating the differences. It will help you with your parenting skills in light of understanding yourself, your style of parenting based on your unique personality, and your children's unique personalities and their needs. It will make your team building successful by teaching you how to employ special easy tools to identify your associates so you are able to give them what they need, want, and value as they work. (See the bibliography for CRGleader and their tools).[5]

May God bless you in your uniqueness. Remember to bless others with who you are as you seek to understand and give others what they need, so your credibility goes up and you are able to be an effective communicator.

Chapter 12

CREDIBILITY YOU CAN BANK ON

"A false witness will perish, but a careful listener will testify successfully." —**Proverbs 21:28,** (NLT)

"...not looking to your own interests, but each of you to the interests of others."
—**Philippians 2:4,** (NIV)

"Be kind and compassionate to one another, forgiving each other, just as in Christ (God) forgave you." —**Ephesians 4:32,** (NIV)

Vocal application: *Your credibility depends on your understanding of the audience, person, or persons in front of you. As a speaker, you must be credible and believable, or you will not have the influence and impact you desire with that* *audience, whether it be one or many. To be believable, you must be full of presence and aware of the needs and values of your audience. Occasionally there will be a heckler in your audience. What do you do? You choose to be kind, respectful, and forgiving toward them. Stay grounded and ask God for His wisdom at that moment rather than feeling panic as to how to respond. It is amazing that usually the person just needs to know you care and that you are listening to them and want to resolve their issue, perhaps at the next break. Being kind and credible works wonders. Is credibility important to voice? It is if you want to shine and present with brilliance, have impact on others, and change the world for the better! As you speak from grounded authenticity, heart, and passion, through your clear open voice with clarity and natural humor, you can affect your world and those in it in an effective, good, and loving or grace-giving way.*

To restate a truth, how can you build up or be a blessing to the other person if you don't know what will bless them? We usually keep trying to give them what **we** want them to hear versus what **they** need to hear, want to hear, and value hearing.

What is credibility? Dictionary.com, LLC says that credibility is the "quality of being believable or worthy of trust."

Being believable and trusted are qualities that are vital to relationship building. Speaking is all about relationship building. Your audience must feel as though you are a trusted friend for you to have any influence with them. When the person or persons in front of you, at any given time, believe you and believe you have their best interest at heart, a relationship is begun and strengthened. The Bible has some advice here.

> *"A false witness will be cut off, but a credible witness will be allowed to speak."* —Proverbs 21:28, (NIV)

You must be credible to be able to speak with influence. Credibility is simply what others see and believe about you. If you are credible when you speak, people will listen. Credibility gives you the power to be heard and valued as a trusted advisor. When you have credibility, others will value what you value, believe what you believe, support your plans, help you achieve your goals, be honest with you, and trust you.

The things and behaviors that build credibility are: honesty, devotion, punctuality, being a good example, ethical behavior, taking responsibility for behavior, keeping promises, forgiving and understanding, getting involved, and focusing on the positive.[5]

Things that destroy credibility are: dishonesty, lack of devotion, being late, being a bad example, non-ethical behavior (lying, cheating, stealing, etc.), not taking responsibility for your behavior, breaking promises, not forgiving or not attempting to understand with compassion, not getting involved, and focusing on the negative.

Are you beginning to see why this attribute called credibility is so vital to you as a speaker?

I borrowed a great acronym called **HAIL** from Julian Treasure. When you speak with Honesty, Authenticity, Integrity, and Love, you become very credible. The seven deadly sins of a speaker that destroy credibility as shared by Julian Treasure are: complaining, dogmatism, exaggeration, excuses, gossip, judging, and negativity. When you understand and speak from the place of **HAIL** (Honesty, Authenticity, Integrity, and Love), you help yourself immensely as a speaker to be credible and trustworthy.

> *"Whoever pursues righteousness and unfailing love will find life, righteousness, and honor."* — Proverbs 21:21, (NIV)

In Other Words, Pursue HAIL as a Speaker and Receive Life, Honor, and Credibility.

One of the things that helps you become credible in the eyes of another is the ability to understand their value system. As good as the many psychological personality profiles are for helping you understand yourself and possibly someone else and their needs, I have found a new and quicker way to understand and value another person so as to be very credible with them. That is the BANKcode methodology of **values and buying behavior**, which is personality based, people focused, and profit and purpose driven.

I can understand my husband's psychological need to have quiet and not be around a lot of people, but if I accidentally step on a deeply held value, such as his value of needing structure or budget competence, I have risked my credibility at that moment, and an argument may ensue. Understanding the value systems of people is very important in credibility. My husband may understand I need to know he thinks I am cute and darling, but if my need to be flexible and have freedom is not met, and I am being forced into his box of perception and thinking, his credibility is damaged in my mind at that moment and must be rebuilt. Of course, my job is to forgive offenses and understand his motivation at that moment, so I can be at peace with him.

> *"Don't look out for your own interests, but take an*
> *interest in others, too."* —Philippians 2:4, (NIV)

I have always emphasized the importance of values along with the psychological personality profile, because it can be like walking in a mine field if you do not understand a person's highest values. You can understand emotional and psychological needs, and yet you can still step on a value mine and **blow up** the relationship at that moment!

When I first saw the BANKcode values based system, I thought it was all messed up, because the descriptive words for the personalities were in different places than I was accustomed to seeing with the psychological personality profiles. The words did not line up with the psychological personality division of needs at all. Then it dawned on me that the words were based on *VALUES* and not psychological needs. The lights came on for me, and I pursued this value-based system to better understand it, so I could give more value to my audiences and clients. I have learned to create my messages to include the basic **BANKcode values** of all four personalities as well as psychological personality needs as discussed in chapter 11. It is amazing how your influence and credibility go sky high with this knowledge.

Most people will not take the time to learn the psychological profiles well enough to be able to identify a client or family member quickly. But the value-based BANKcode system allows you to obtain insight with lightning speed because the client or family member readily knows their values and identifies them for you in ninety seconds or less. The BANKcode system gives you the answer to why people buy you or your product or service *Why They Buy* is the new book by Cheri Tree, CEO of BANKcode. In this new book, Cheri answers the question of why people buy into you and your product or service. She shares the statistics from the Chally Group that show that only eighteen percent of buyers will buy from a salesperson who does not match the buyer's personality type versus eighty-two percent success when personality types are aligned.[6]

Go to www.mybankcode.com/CLStanley for better understanding and the ability to identify your code of values for yourself. At this web address you will find a gift for you from me, as I am a certified and licensed trainer in this BANKcode methodology. Should you like to look further, go to www.bankcode.com and put in the access code CLStanley to receive best pricing on the VT training offered there.

The buying values-based system is as follows: The **B** of BANK stands for **Blueprint** and defines the values as follows: stability, structure, systems, planning, processes, predictability, responsibility, rules, credentials, duty, titles, and traditions. The Blueprint is comfortable "in the box."

The **A** in BANK stands for **Action** with these values: freedom, flexibility, fun, spontaneity, stimulation, action, attention, competition, excitement, image, opportunity, and winning. The Action person is "out of the box."

The **N** in BANK stands for **Nurturing** with these values: relationships, authenticity, charity, contribution, community, ethics, harmony, involvement, morality, personal growth, significance, and teamwork. The Nurturer "decorates and recycles the box."

The **K** in BANK represents **Knowledge** with these values: learning, accuracy, competence, expertise, intelligence, logic, research and development, science, self mastery, technology, the big picture, and universal truths. The Knowledge person "invented the box."

Now I don't want you to feel confused with this new information as to the BANKcode buying values versus the psychological personality profile needs and values. I often get asked, "Isn't this just another personality profile like all the rest? The answer is: **it is exactly the same only completely different.** They both help you to identify yourself, clients, audience, or family. It helps significantly to have an understanding of both the personality profile based on psychology, like the many out there all coming from the original work of Hippocrates; and the BANKcode values of the personalities that are grouped a bit differently, designed around sales. The main reason I am sharing BANKcode with you is that it is easy, fast, and accurate in helping you be more effective as a communicator. You do not need someone to take a questionnaire or have to go into depth to be able to identify and know how to communicate well with them. The BANKcode system has been scientifically proven to be effective in communication and accurately predicts buying behavior. In a scientific study done by San Francisco State University in 2016, a scientific white paper was produced and can be viewed at www.bankcode.com/CLStanley.

We all are in sales in life, would you not agree? You sold yourself to your parents with your desires for Christmas. You sold yourself to your mate or partner in life. You sell yourself daily to the people in your circle of influence. So the fact that BANKcode is a proven predictor of "buy-ology," it truly helps your credibility and effectiveness in communication with the people in your life.

As a speaker, you must know the keys to the four sets of BANKcode values, as well as the previously shared psychological personality needs of your audience.

So it all boils down to knowing the importance of psychological need of fun and influence for the Affective, speaking and bringing the point home quickly for the Behavioral, yet detailed enough to satisfy the psychological need of the Cognitive person, and easy to remember and understand points in your speech for the Interpersonal. But also the BANKcode values for the BLUEPRINT who needs and values structure, budgets, planning, and systems; ACTIONS need freedom and stardom or being treated very specially and with fast action; NURTURERS need and value heartfelt importance of helping people and the planet, authenticity, and relationships; and the KNOWLEDGE person who needs and values budgets, science and technology, learning, and the big picture.

So when you are speaking to an audience, in your sixty-second commercial, you must include the fact that you or your program is **affordable**, that you offer a **system** and a **plan**, that there is **science** behind you, that the **planet is a better place** because of your ideals, and that **fast action** happens with you, so they can realize their desire to be **important** and of **star** quality. All these things and/ or any other of the BANKcode values must be communicated to attract the whole room. Just be sure all four value sets are touched on in any presentation no matter how short or long.

Your credibility is of huge importance. The need to be respected as having something of worth to give to others, and their perception that they should listen to what you have to say, is extremely important to you as a speaker or singer. Use your amazing personality and value systems based on BANKcode as well as the psychological needs to increase your credibility in all situations.

A quick story of why your credibility in family is important. A Bankcode trainer was visiting a family of friends, and decided to offer the easy and fun BANKcode value cards to them for a quick assessment. The mother, father, and daughter of the family, in less than ninety seconds, showed their cards stacked up with red Action cards on top with their green Knowledge cards on the bottom, and with a variance as to how their Nurture and Blueprints stacked. The son stacked his value cards with the Knowledge on top and his red Action card on the bottom. Why this is so significant is that the son was considering suicide because he felt so different, and as though he didn't fit in anywhere, especially in his family. When asked what he thought, he said, "After looking at the BANK cards, I realize there is **nothing** wrong with me. I am just a high Knowledge guy, while you all are high Red Actions. And for your info, I know more than all of you put together!"

He no longer considered suicide as he now understood why he had felt he was a misfit. He now understood he was designed by God differently with high intelligence and love for learning as a high Knowledge guy, while the rest of his family's values were more Action oriented. Now that they understood each other better, their credibility with each other was increased dramatically. As a result, their relationships were greatly improved.

Example of Non-credible Behavior from a Person Who Calls Herself Christian

I want to tell you a quick story of an example of credibility going bad.

My daughter works in a large hospital that focusses on helping families with children who are very ill and often dying. Two women came into the hospital with gift bags for the families in the hospital. One woman was a young mother with a tiny baby in her arms, and the other woman was an older woman. They did not stop to ask questions, but proceeded to walk down a hall to patient rooms.

My daughter, who is a devout Christ follower and was at the desk, stopped them nicely and let them know that there were very ill children on that floor and that the young mother should not risk exposing her tiny baby to the dangers in that particular hall. The older woman was surprised at being stopped and was quite insistent on letting my daughter know she was a Christian and there were Bibles and Christian oriented gifts in the bags. She was insistent and intent on giving the gift bags to all the rooms. My daughter explained that giving these bags to everyone would violate the hospital policies regarding these types of gifts. She asked if the ladies would consider leaving the gift bags, and allow the hospital spiritual advisor to distribute the bags to the families they would truly serve.

The older woman became indignant and stormed out with her bags in tow. She returned later when my daughter was not at the desk. In fact, no one saw her come in and head down the hall, where she distributed a list to all the families of the gift bag contents. When my daughter and the people in charge discovered what had taken place, it was distressing, and worse than if they had given the bags out. Her actions totally and intentionally violated the hospital policies, staff's wishes, and exhibited general lack of human kindness and understanding.

My question is this: was the woman's credibility as a Christian intact? NO! She totally destroyed her credibility. People saw her as a person who could not be trusted with truth, or the rules and policies of the hospital. She was viewed as "another crummy Christian" in the eyes of the hospital administration. She was not only giving herself a bad name with no credibility, but she was giving Jesus a bad name because of her choice to let others know and flaunt her Christian status. She chose to behave in a self-righteous way, doing what she wanted to do, choosing to not understand the reasons behind the hospital policies or honor them with loving intention.

Behaving congruently with who you claim to be is so important for credibility. Jesus calls us to love and respect one another with understanding, compassion, and kindness. This woman totally destroyed that end.

Credible Worship Groups

I want to speak to church worship bands and singers because their endeavors need to be perceived as credible and professional. When worship bands and singers lead congregations in worship music, what do you see and experience? I hope you see all ages working together, young and old. I hope you see them all dressed respectfully for stage, so as the congregation looks up on an angle, they are not distracted by tight and ill-fitting slacks and skirts that are too short or too long for stage. Be careful of full-length skirts. For some shorter women, the long skirt squashes you and makes you appear short and stubby. Remember, skirts that reach mid-knee or just below the knee are the most flattering on your body. They work well for stage platform, which always makes your garments appear shorter.

Guys should be in ironed, well-groomed shirts, slacks, and possibly sweaters, vests, or jackets. Are you trustworthy as a worship leader? Your dress and total demeanor say either you are credible and trustworthy or not (see chapter 9).

Your job as a worship leader is to bring the people into the throne room of God's grace with you. They have come in with the weight of the world on their shoulders. You arrived early and dropped your worldly weight at the door with the power of prayer and by seeking God with your whole heart. Now that you are "prayed up" and rehearsed, you are ready to invite all who come into the sanctuary to join you in worship. Eye contact with your congregants or audience is important. It is key for credible connection. It is important to express a kind and inviting attitude through your eyes by meeting theirs.

Be present, for that is where God shows up—in the present. Too many worship leaders close their eyes and cut themselves off from the congregants during the whole worship session. Ask yourself **why** you are doing what you are doing? Why are you closing your eyes? As I have trained worship groups, I have found the real reason for closing eyes is mostly because you do not want to deal with your nervousness as others are looking at you. I know you stand behind the idea of worshipping God in your own way. But your job on platform is to **engage**, not hide.

How do you feel as a worshiper in the congregation? Do you feel invited to enter into the worship with the leaders? Are they credible? Or do you feel cut off and on your own because the eye contact is not there? Doesn't it feel good when leaders invite you to join them in worshipping, as if friends are meeting and greeting you as you join together to worship the Lord?

I know you want to close your eyes and sing to God, but be careful to stay engaged with a credible attitude that expresses togetherness when on the worship platform. Remember to connect with God in your heart and the people in the congregation with connected credible actions of engagement and authentic caring about them. Eye contact is critically important in this setting, as it is in any stage, speaking or singing setting. Remember, you must know why you are doing what you are doing in all situations where you are communicating with others. Be present and connected, always!

In most churches today a gulf or physical separation (a platform or stage) stands between the worship leader or team and the congregants. This gulf or big space, where the orchestra would be in a theater, cuts off or separates you on stage from the audience or congregation. By virtue of the physical setting, or context, an environment and culture of stage performers and passive audience has arisen. As worship singers or speakers, you must reach across that gulf and invite or engage your audience in what is happening. They must be engaged with eyes and hearts and attitudes of credible invitation to join you in worship and praise of God.

What does it mean to perform? In Dictionary.com the definition is: to carry out, to accomplish, to succeed in doing. What are you trying to do or accomplish? Do you desire to do your best work for God and His people? I hope you truly want to accomplish, deliver well, and do your best or "perform" as a Godly worship leader.

Some recoil at the word "entertain." But Dictionary.com says to entertain is: "to hold the attention of pleasantly or agreeably, to have a guest—show hospitality to." In other words, "entertain" or invite them in with you as you invite Christ in.

You are stepping up in excellence and **performing** a great service to your congregation as they come in hassled, tired from the night before, and perhaps after just having an argument with a spouse or family member. You must **show** up, **pray** up, and be ready to **perform** your best duty to **invite** them and hospitibly **entertain** or invite them and **Christ** with you in this musical expression we call worship.

It is always about giving your audience what they need from you as a credible servant to bless them and give them value.

Handshakes Matter!

After you speak and/or sing, you will want to converse with the people in your

audience or congregation. Your handshake is important to meet and greet people. Open your hand and meet the other hand by locking thumbs (your thumb curve goes into their thumb curve). As you gently start to grip their hand, you can feel how much pressure they give you as you gently squeeze their hand with the same pressure they are giving you. This is a good handshake that conveys you **know who you are** by the thumb lock, but **you care about them** with the careful squeeze, which indicates you are paying attention to them and listening to their bodily squeeze needs. This kind of a handshake is a credibility builder.

Nothing is worse than the "limp fish" handshake, where you appear not to know who you are and really don't care about meeting the other person, since your fingers barely touch and you have no thumb lock. Equally annoying is the "power grip" handshake, where you come on too strong and "kill" the other person's hand, which makes you appear to be overbearing and noncaring, thus noncredible. Men tend to do both these, either the limp fish for fear of hurting a woman, or the latter power grip that is too much for many men and women.

When you move in with an open thumb and lock with them and feel for an equal squeeze, you share yourself and really connect with the other person. Be sure and look them in the eye and smile genuinely and warmly. You are now credibly connected.

Again, your attitude is "king." Remember your spirit creates your thoughts, which are tied to your emotions, which lead to beliefs and attitudes, which change brain and body chemistry and lead to behavior. An attitude of gratitude takes you far in all situations. Love and gratitude are always appreciated and credible. Think more of the other person than yourself and keep a loving thankful attitude at all times. The attitude of gratitude will always serve you well!

What if You Woke Up Today with Only What You Were Consciously Thankful for Yesterday?

That is a powerful question and one to ponder well. Think about this question and make a list of ten things you are thankful for right now. Do this every day and see how your world changes for the better. Remember, you could wake up tomorrow with it all gone if you were not thankful for it today. What you appreciate gets better. What is depreciated gets worse and potentially goes away!

One morning I was upset with my husband. As I made the bed I jerked the bed covers up and thought how justified I was with my upset attitude. Then a voice came on the radio telling me to stop and choose to think of all the things about my mate that I loved and for which I was thankful. The voice also said, "Even if you think you married the wrong mate, God can make them the right mate." That got my attention. While it was a very difficult thing to do at that moment, I decided to take on the challenge.

As I began to really conjure up why I loved this man (I had to really conjure hard in this angry moment), an amazing thing happened. My emotions shifted dramatically from anger to love, and my whole body began to relax. By choosing to actively think of good and change my attitude with my thoughts, an attitude of thankfulness became easy. Truth showed up again for me. I did love him, do love him, and I am thankful for him. Finishing making the bed was calm and easy. I had to sit down and ask God to forgive me for my bad attitude. The interesting thing about thankfulness is that it begets more thankfulness. I was now aware of so much more for which I was thankful, not only my husband, but my children, friends, extended family, my home, and even my bed! I woke up the next day still married, as I am today, with all the above and more.

Do you think I was more credible with him and others with an attitude of thankfulness? Yes!

Here is another story about gratitude and how our spirits, minds, and bodies connect and bless us. I was walking around the block at home feeling kind of grumpy and physically crummy. Have you ever been there? I chose to act and walk rather than waiting to be motivated first. I know that **action creates motivation** and helps me do what is right. As I walked, my mind went to the words of a song I loved to sing. The song reminded me that when you "Praise the Lord, He can work through those who praise Him, Praise the Lord, for our God inhabits praise..." It occurred to me as I walked, that if I began praising God and thanking Him for all He is and all He has made and done, He actually might physically inhabit my praise. Well, as I walked, praised, and was thankful, all of a sudden I began to feel the physical warmth of the Holy Spirit engulf me. My physical state changed radically from lousy and weak to strong, joyful, and very thankful!

I had felt this Holy Spirit habitation before when the Holy Spirit gave me my special Holy Spirit song language, when my youngest son was born, when I was hearing shocking life-altering news, and when my first grandson was born. God showed up and changed my world of spirit, mind, and body. God's Spirit moved through my spirit first, then my mind, brain, and body. All you need to know is to say "yes" to God as you choose to believe, and show an attitude of gratitude and praise, and wow! He really shows up.

Remember You Will Always Be a Great and Credible Speaker or Singer If You:

- Look to and seek God first in all your endeavors.

- Own your message as if from the very throne room of God. If speaking, make a mind map of your key points that include BANKcode values and psychological triggering words for all four personality value systems. Just as a singer paints pictures with his or her lyrics, speakers must do the same with words. Take in your message and internalize it so you now own it. When you have internalized the message and own it as yours, you now have a gift to give from your heart and experience. It will not only bless the audience, but it will bring praise back to God and complete the big circle of ministry, and bless your socks off!

- Put yourself together with a professional wardrobe, hair, and make-up intact.

- Stand tall in stature with an imaginary bungee cord in place, being grounded and with a great attitude of gratitude.

- Anchor yourself in a high state of loving, joyful, thankful emotion and "I can't wait to go out there and give my gift" enthusiasm ready to give your audience the gift of you from your heart.

- Clothe yourself with Colossians clothes of compassion, kindness, humility (agreeing with God as to who you are), gentleness, patience, and, over all, love.

- Remember to deliver from your authentic heart through well-rehearsed, open, and focused vocal systems. See your mind map or your song in your mind and give away your message or song as your best gift from your heart.

184

Chapter 13

LIFE OF PURPOSE, WHY AM I HERE?

*"For I know the plans I have for you, says the Lord.
They are plans for good and not for disaster, (to
give you a future and a hope). In those days when
you pray, I will listen. If you look for me whole-
heartedly, you will find Me."*

—**Jeremiah 29:11–13**, (NIV)

Vocal Application: *We tend to, at times, feel
in captivity to fear of failure or fear of success.
People fear public speaking more than they fear
death. The US statistics state that sixty-eight percent of people fear death, and seventy-four percent fear public speaking. God has a plan and a
purpose within you to bring Him glory through
you, and make you joyful and fulfilled. You, as
a speaker or singer, are your happiest and best*

when you discover and implement the plans God has for you. Keep seeking Him and He will answer you in miraculous ways. Doors of opportunity tend to open when you project yourself in a real and passionate way to others. Never try to be a copy of anyone other than the real beautiful and awesome you.

W hat a great way to begin a chapter on God's purpose in you. He truly has a purpose in creating you and putting a wonderful spirit in you (the real you) that was designed to be joined to His Spirit so you will truly prosper and have hope and a future! His Word is so encouraging to me. It lifts me up and puts me back on my feet when I am in a quandary about anything.

What is purpose? Dictionary.com, LLC says: "Purpose is the reason for which something exists or is done, made, used, etc."

God says in the Bible that His purpose prevails in you:

> *"Many are the plans in a person's heart, but it is the Lord's purpose that prevails."* — Proverbs 19:21, (NIV)

> *"In his heart a man plans his course, but the Lord determines his steps."* — Proverbs 1:9, (NIV)

The reason for which you exist and were made is God's idea. In other Scriptures it also says your purpose is to bring God glory in all you are, do, and say.

In Pastor Rick Warren's book, *The Purpose Driven Life*, he asks a question right up front: "What am I here for?" A great question and one that we all have asked of ourselves at times.

As a budding or professional speaker or singer, you must know the answer to this question. You must be in touch with the gift in you that is designed to bless the world. You cannot hide your thoughts and intentions from your audience. No matter how great your words are, the heart intent, authentic desire, and intention will show through your words. Remember, the heart intent is so much louder than the words themselves.

"So how do I answer the question "why am I here?," you may be asking?

You must know who you are, Whose you are, and that you have a destiny as discussed in chapters 1-5 and beyond. And you must get in touch with how God uniquely put you together with your spirit, mind, body, personality, abilities, gifting, talents, and experiences. (See Personality and Credibility in chapters, 11 and 12.)

Seek God and ask Him, because He promises in His Word to listen and hear you, and, more importantly, He answers you by bringing you out of the captivity and confusion of your own mind. When you listen to the world around you, you get confused as to who you are and lose touch with your unique purpose God placed in you at conception and birth.

If you are asking and seeking God, He will assure you are on the right path. Listen to Him and less to your doubts. He is leading you along the way He has planned for you regardless of poor life choices.

As Dr. Caroline Leaf says in her book, *Switch on Your Brain,*[2] you always have a choice to choose healthy thinking versus toxic thinking. God calls you to "choose life and blessing."

> *"I call Heaven and Earth to witness against you today: I place before you Life and Death, Blessing and Curse. Choose life so that you and your children will live. Love God, your God, listening obediently to him, firmly embracing him. Oh yes, he is life itself..."* —Deuteronomy 30:19, (MSG)

> *"I will instruct you and teach you in the way you should go; I will counsel you with my loving eye on you."* —Psalm 32:8, (NIV)

> *"God saved you by his grace when you believed. And you can't take credit for this; it is a gift from God. Salvation is not a reward for the good things we have done, so none of us can boast about it. For we are God's masterpiece. He has created us anew in Christ Jesus, so we can do the good things he planned for us long ago."* —Ephesians 2:8–10, (NLT)

I have come to know and understand that your purpose consists of your unique way of being a child of God, as He connects with your spirit in the "Tree of Excellence" (chapters 3 and 5). But also your purpose is derived from your unique way of thinking in your excellent mind (chapter 6), being in your excellent body (chapter 7), your personality (chapters 11 and 12) as well as natural abilities, gifting, and life experiences. By looking at these things you will start to see what God had in mind for you when He created you in your mother's womb. All of these elements make up the unique **you.** They are all important to understand as a speaker and presenter, because you must know yourself and your purpose to be able to truly give your special gift of you to others.

Let's use the "Tree of Excellence," **Spirit, Mind, Body** plus the acronym of **PAGE** for what "page of life" you are on to explain your purpose. The first thing you must deal with is your Spirit as in chapter 5. God places special spiritual gifts in you to be used to lift up, support, and influence people for good everywhere, but especially those in your family and life relationships, including the greater body of believers, His church. The church is meant to inspire, support, and equip you, as a believer in Jesus Christ, to be everything God designed for you to be in order to bring glory to Himself, to bring the truth of Jesus to the world, and to contribute to making the world a better place to live. There can be misunderstanding of these gifts, but God gives us these gifts for the benefit of all.

There are twenty-five gifts in all according to the Ministry Resource Center (mintools.com), and they are found in several passages of the Bible. Some are found in passages other than the traditional ones that explain spiritual gifting, but the point is that God gives special gifts to each one of us to be used to help others and build them up. God blesses each one of us with natural gifting, but when you know Jesus and have the benefit of the power of the Holy Spirit operating within you, the natural gifts you have been given become enhanced and even more useful and beneficial to humanity. I like to call them gifts on God's steroids!

You can find the gifts in the following Bible references: 1 Corinthians 12:8–12, 28–30; Romans 12:6–8; Ephesians 3:6–8, 4:11; 1 Peter 4:9–10.

The Scripture says it best as to why there are spiritual gifts and the uniqueness of them to the body, the church. The Bible clearly states that these gifts are given to you by the Holy Spirit of God for the common good and edification of you and others in the church. So when you choose to believe in Christ, you get the added benefit of having the Holy Spirit within your spirit, with a new awareness and power attached to your natural God-given gifts.

So the first part of finding your purpose in the "Tree of Excellence" is the top of the tree, or **Spirit** area of your life. This is where you discover what it means to be a child of God and experience all your relationships with others and giving of your fruit (chapter 5).

The next part of your "Tree of Excellence" is your **Mind** (chapter 6). God has given you a unique way to think and understand life. You have an intellect, emotions, and a will. You must feed your mind with nutrients of God enlightenment. You can choose your thoughts, taking captive thoughts that do not serve you or others, and replace the toxic thoughts with positive truth. As you renew your mind daily with positive truth from the Bible, you become more and more in touch with the purpose God placed uniquely in you. You truly begin to transform.

The other important root area for feeding you, the "Tree of Excellence," is your unique **Body**. God does not make mistakes, and your body is uniquely yours, and is part of your purpose. We all have a tendency to want to change something about our bodies. But God's call to you is to be a great caretaker of the body He gave you. Some of you are gifted in and love physical beauty, some are athletically gifted, and some think you missed the boat all together! The truth is, there is no such thing as a human who is not beautiful and very special with great purpose.

You must take care of your body and be healthy as discussed in chapter 7. And, as part of your overall health, you must know how to clean, groom, and dress your body to be able to fulfill your purpose to its fullest (chapter 9).

*"People look at the outer appearance, but the Lord
looks at the heart."* — 1 Samuel 16:7, (NIV)

You are *fearfully and wonderfully made* to reflect God's appearance. Your purpose that He planned for you is reflected in your physicality as well as your mind, and spirit.

The acronym PAGE stands for Personality, Abilities, Gifts, and Experiences. Personality, as explained in chapters 11 and 12, is discussed and is important to your unique purpose. God gave you a unique personality, or way of behaving and way of processing thought. These aspects of your life color how you see the world and how you relate to it. They are vital to your unique God-given purpose and help you understand your credibility.

P is for **Personality**, but also for **Passion**. What is your passion or passions? What was in God's mind when He made you? What things in society or problems bother you the most? When you get on your soap box, what do you say? If you could do anything with no restraints of time or money, what would you do? These are all questions to ask yourself to help you connect with your passions and God's purpose in you. Answer these questions below.

"*Where there is no vision, the people perish: but he that keeps the law, happy is he.*"—Proverbs 29:18, (KJV)

You must be able to dream and envision doing and being all God designed for you to be and do. Dreaming is often nearly lost when you reach adulthood. It seems life just gets in the way of your dreams and you forget them, or allow them to become so foggy that you don't see them anymore. As the passage says, without your vision or dreams you literally seem to perish or die.

Tied to your dreams and passion is your heart. Your heart is where God speaks to you as discussed in chapter 6. What is it you do that makes your heart happy and causes it to "sing"? For me it is singing, speaking, teaching, training others, and coaching them to be their best at communicating well so that their hearts can sing and bless others. What is it for you?

What did you love to do as a child? What were your big dreams of what you wanted to be or do when you grew up? A clue to your purpose is to look at what you loved as a child. Have you ever heard the old saying, "If you do what you love for a career, it is never work?" When you love doing something, it makes your heart "sing" with joy, even when challenges come. Because you love what you do, you find solutions to challenges with more ease. **In fact, the more problems you have, the happier you are because problems create value.** When you solve a problem, you feel great and obtain more credibility and are valued more.

The bigger your dreams, the bigger your problems, but the more fun you have solving them and experiencing the benefits that come from pushing through the challenge.

Ask yourself about your dreams all through your life and write them down. Take a careful look and allow yourself to begin to "feel" the hope of those dreams again in your mind and body. How does it feel? Your answer should be a clue as to your God-given purpose. Answer the questions asked of you in the above three paragraphs. What makes your heart sing? What did you love to do as a child? What did you want to be when you grew up? When you feel God's pleasure in you, what are you doing?

_____

_____

_____

_____

_____

As I embraced the challenge to do this, I found that I came alive inside as I thought about the dream of performing at Carnegie Hall in New York, which represented for me influencing a great number of people. Even though I did not sing at Carnegie, I saw that as life got in my way, God allowed me to, in fact, influence a great many people for good with all He has allowed me to do as I raised my family and kept pursuing my "heart singing" activities and loves.

Maybe you want or wanted to be a great speaker. Here you are reading this book and gaining some insight as to how to better do that. I challenge and encourage you to pursue your "heart-singing" activities. Where there is a will, there is always a way. God will make a way!

The next elements of your purpose PAGE are your **Abilities**. If you are like most of the human race, you have many abilities— some in-born and some you have developed. Your strengths, skills, natural talents, careers, jobs, what others say you are good at, what makes you feel good or great about yourself, what you loved doing as a child, and what has been the most meaningful parts of your past are all clues to your abilities and purpose. All these are things to consider and write down. When you think about and write out your thoughts, you see things more clearly. Write your strengths, skills, talents, jobs you have been good at, things that people say you are good at, what makes you feel great about yourself when you do it, your beloved childhood activities, etc.

_____

_____

_____

_____

_____

When I have done this exercise of writing down the things I have suggested to you, it helped make my abilities more clear, and it helped me see the ones that mean the most to me. I am creative and can sew well. I love to design challenging garments like wedding or evening gowns, etc. I love to draw and paint. I am a creative and good cook. I can take on just about anything and do it well, when asked. I am good at acting, singing, modeling, directing, and speaking. This could be a curse, having many abilities. But I have discovered, while I am good at many things, I am great at and love to speak, sing, coach, train, and encourage others to act, model, sing, and speak well with excellence. Focusing on what I am great at has cleared the clutter of trying to do too many things, taking me away from my best purpose. Being good at many things can be the enemy of the **great** in you, your true purpose.

It can take a lifetime to figure it all out, but I encourage you to never stop. I encourage you to take seriously writing down of all your abilities, and then assess which ones you love **most.**

The next element of PAGE is **Gifts**. Along with your abilities are your gifts and talents. God used your parents and all your ancestors to create your unique gifts and talents in you. Some people can fold their tongues, while others cannot. As a voice teacher and student of speech and sound production physiology, I recognize the uniqueness of voice student's physical gifting. For some, the dished tongue response comes more naturally than others, for instance; or vibrato shows up immediately for some while others must discover it as they train and learn to release it as they sing well.

The good news is that regardless of your physical gifting, you can learn and strengthen the responses that create wonderful dished tongue, full sound, and vibrato. But the fact that some come to the physical and auditory responses more naturally leaves many to believe there are those who have a singing talent or gift and those who don't. What I know and have proven for years is that if you have a strong love and God-given desire to sing, for instance, you can learn the physical and auditory responses and learn to sing. The ability to identify pitch and sing can be developed at any age. God says we can all make a joyful "noise," or sound for His glory. The noise He refers to is not dissonant noise as we think of it, but a beautiful sound to His ears. Remember, you have abilities and gifts to be used well in your purpose.

Your gifts and talents, no matter what they are, become enhanced when you allow the Holy Spirit of God to enter the gift and show you how best to use it for His glory and the benefit of mankind. Just know everyone is gifted with talents and uniqueness of gifting. If you are not sure about yours, I encourage you to go back and answer the questions previously asked in this chapter.

The final element of PAGE is your **Experience**. You have had and will continue to have unique experiences in life. These may include your birth and circumstances surrounding it, your family of origin birth order, family, teachers, trauma, what you regret doing or not fully doing, being or having and why, your self-image and esteem, what you perceive held you back, etc. Again, I ask you to think deeply and carefully about your experiences and look for God's "lemonade" (good outcome) instead of the lemons (pain). Write down your insights and thoughts. Look for ways your experiences set you apart in a good way, and all that can come out of them for pulling you toward your true dreams and purpose. Your unique messages quite often come out of life experiences. Those that challenged you most helped you trust God the most, and create the biggest blessing to others. Remember, God wastes nothing that happens to you in your life.

The hurts or trauma in life can be our biggest blessing as a speaker. It is when we share our "skinned knees" of life, so to speak, that we gain more credibility with others. You often find connection to passion as you reflect on your life experiences, good, bad, and in between. We only grow in the valleys of life, not the mountain-tops. Write your experiences and positive thoughts around them, thus identifying how your experience might comfort someone else. (see 2 Corinthians 1:3–6)

_____

_____

_____

_____

_____

_____

_____

As a speaker, credibility is vital. What is credibility? As mentioned in chapter 12, it is the level of respect others think about you. As your credibility of expertise and vulnerability increases, so does others' willingness to: believe what you believe, value what you value, support your plans, help you achieve your goals, be honest with you, and trust you.[5]

When you speak, you are sharing a gift within you or a cause that you are passionate about. Do you care if they believe you or want to support you? Of course you do! Your purpose and credibility are wrapped up in your behavior and passion.

A great exercise is to write your eulogy. Write what you want others to say at your passing on to heaven. This is a great exercise in getting in touch with your purpose and why you are here. Allow it to be a good insight to the deeper you.

I want others to "get" who I am and my heart's desire of wanting only the best for others. I want to do good and leave only good for others who follow after me in this life. My love of Jesus and who He is means the most to me. My family and those relationships that God has allowed me to have are vital to me. I truly love other people, even those who have hurt me deeply. And I want my clients to have my best so that they can thrive in life.

My eulogy would go something like this: *Carol was a woman who loved God with her whole heart and, as a result, loved all those with whom she came in contact. She cared deeply for her family and spent many years cherishing her husband, children, and grandchildren, and caring for her parents in their late seventies, eighties, and nineties. She was driven to use her gifts and talents to share her multiplicity of expertise, knowledge, and love of God with others, and the vital connection of all the above to true success in life. She always believed in her family, friends, and clients, and made them feel supported, encouraged, and that they were significant and "awesome." We will miss her enthusiasm for life, warm smile, hugs, and joyful loving attitude we all felt when with her.*

Do your own assessment of what matters to you, and then write your own eulogy.

_____

_____

_____

_____

_____

Another element of your purpose is understanding what God might have been thinking when He created you with all your special uniqueness. After going through all these exercises of writing out all the elements of your *"Tree of Excellence"* SMB-PAGE and your eulogy, are you beginning to see the beauty of all He has allowed in your life? All you are and have in your spirit, mind, body, personality, ability, gifting, and experience give you a glimpse of God's thoughts and plans for you. I want to go to heaven and have Him say, "Well done, my good and faithful servant!" I never want to live with regret. I used to worry that someday in heaven God would show me all I missed or could have done and experienced if I had chosen differently in life. I now know that is toxic thinking. So, I choose to move forward and not look back with any "what if" thoughts. I only have today and what I choose to do with it. You only have today, and what is before you this day comes with new mercies every morning. Yesterday is gone and **history**. Tomorrow is a **mystery** and not here yet. You only have now, which is the present moment. God meets you in this present moment, which is a **gift**, thus called the **"present."** Make the most joyful use of this present moment and day with God supporting you and leading you forward to continue to fulfill His purpose in you.

Chapter 14

SEEING BALANCE MATTERS

"But seek first his kingdom and his righteousness, and all these things will be given to you as well."
—Matthew 6:33, (NIV)

Vocal application: *For you to be at peace and achieve any sense of balance you must be able to see yourself as the "Tree of Excellence" and be sure you are getting all you need so you can keep bearing fruit to give to others. While some believe balance is impossible, I believe you are always in flux as you attempt to stay relatively in balance in order to function well. A clear picture of who you are as a triune person, an understanding of why you are here or your purpose, in balance with vocal techniques, professionalism, understanding personality, and all other areas of your life are all keys to your speaking and singing. You will*

> *speak out of passion and substance based on all of your life gifts and experiences, good, great and "lemon like" that God turns into lemonade for you to share. Remember God wastes nothing that you experience. As you seek God and the illusive perfection with balance, you actually achieve more balance than you think and serve others better in your communication.*

This chapter is short and sweet. It is in the interdependence and balance of your life, spirit, mind, and body, and the other areas that hold the keys to long life, health, happiness, and great communication as a speaker.

If you go back to look at you, the "Tree of Excellence," in chapter 3, you will see that the spirit, or top of the tree, is dependent on the roots of mind, and body for sustenance, as well as the life-giving "Son-shine" to provide leaves that are always green that produce life energy, blossoms, and fruit at the top of the tree. The root systems are dependent on good soil and life-giving water (what you feed your roots), and the spirit draws the nutrients and water to the top of the tree. They are all interdependent.

The tree image also gives you a way to see if you are reasonably in balance. Are you spending way too much time in your activity and relationships with your work, where you earn your living, and neglecting other relationships? How long has it been since you spoke to certain family members who are clearly shown to you in the family branches of your tree? Are you volunteering and keeping your friendships alive? What are you doing to care for your relationship with yourself by renewing your mind daily? How is your body doing with health, nutrition, water intake, rest, and exercize?

The tree becomes a great gage for you to keep tabs easily on your life balance, keeping in mind that you cannot do everything at once, but are working along at your best for the moment in time with all the needs that life demands. Again, you, as the "Tree of Excellence," are all about relationships with yourself (roots of mind and body care), God and others (the top of the tree), and how they all interact.

Another great picture of balance is the three-legged stool as an example here.

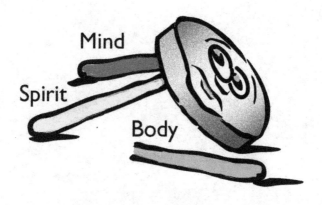

If you have ever used a three-legged stool to sit on, you know that even if the legs are a bit wobbly, it still seats itself and is useful as a stool. But if even one leg is missing, the stool is totally worthless as a sitting device.

You are your voice and your voice is you—all of you. To understand this, the whole of you gives voice to, or broadcasts through, your physical vocal instrument, and who you are in your thoughts, emotions, attitudes, and passions to others. Your spirit affects and helps to create your thoughts, which are joined to emotions. Your thoughts with their attached emotions create brain chemistry and physical dendrite cells. Your brain controls and deeply affects your body and its physical make-up and health. Your thoughts can even Change your DNA, according to Dr. Caroline Leaf.[1,2]

Your spirit affects your mind which affects your brain, which affects your body. They are all interdependent just like the three-legged stool legs are totally interdependent for the stool to be functional. The spirit must be considered dramatically as a pillar "leg"; the mind and brain must together be considered as a pillar "leg"; and the body is a pillar "leg." You cease to exist as a balanced productive human without any one of these "legs," just as the three-legged stool ceases to exist as a functional stool if one leg is broken or gone.

This is very important to understand. Many people think the spirit is not important, only the brain and the body as if only they count for your healthy existence. The truth is your spirit drives you, just as the top of the tree drives the life and miracle fruit it produces. If the roots bring all kinds of good nutrients, carried by the water of life to the tree, but there is no full spectrum sunlight to create the miracle of leaves and photosynthesis, transforming the nutrients and water into life-giving energy and fruit, the tree ceases to exist as a purposeful fruit-bearing and beautiful shade-giving tree.

The same happens to you. Without healthy "Son-light" driven spirits and root nutrients of good input through your five senses and body care, you cease to thrive. Your roots (body and mind) need the Spirit, and the Spirit needs the roots for healthy existence.

What does this have to do with your voice? You (spirit, mind, and body) create and develop your voice, and your physical voice expresses the whole of you—spirit, mind, and body.

You must be aware of your spirit, as it drives your thoughts, brain, and body. Your spirit, when plugged into the Holy Spirit of God through belief and trust in Jesus Christ, will help you change your negative mind stories that keep you from success and purpose. You always have a choice as to who and what you listen to, your negative story, or God's truth of success and purpose. You can choose to take negative story thoughts captive. They are not in your best interest, so choose good healthy thinking, and agree with what God says about you. Speak out loud these statements and feel your joy and confidence rise. While there are many statements of God's love and provision for you in Scriture, here are a few of His truths about you:

I am dearly loved and greatly prized by God—(taken from John 3:16)
I am God's child—(taken from John 1:12)
I am a friend of God—(taken from John 15:15)
I am no longer a slave to sin—(taken from Romans 6:6)
I am accepted by Christ—(taken from Romans 15:7)
God leads me in triumph in Christ—(taken from 2 Corinthians 2:14)
I am a new creation in Christ—(taken from 2 Corinthians 5:17)
I am the righteousness of God in Christ—(taken from 2 Corinthians 5:21)
I am no longer a slave, but an heir—(taken from Galatians 4:7)
I have been blessed with every spiritual blessing in Christ—(taken from Ephesians 1:3)

I am forgiven and redeemed by the grace of Christ—(taken from Ephesians 1:7)

I have a God-given purpose—(taken from Ephesians 1:11)

I am God's masterpiece created in Christ Jesus for good works—(taken from Ephesians 2:10)

My new self is righteous and holy—(taken from Ephesians 4:24)

I was formerly darkness, but now I am light in the Lord—(taken from Ephesians 5:8)

God supplies all of my need—(taken from Philippians 4:19)

I have been made complete in Christ—(taken from Colossians 2:10)

I am holy and dearly loved—(taken from Colossians 3:12)

The more you embrace these truths from Scripture about who you have become in Christ, the more stable, grateful, and fully assured you will be in this world. You become what you believe, and you behave by what you believe.

Renew your mind daily with truth from God's Word and positive influences. Stop listening to cultural messages that "take you out"! Our culture is toxic and toxicity is death to a tree; it kills it. It will kill or stop you at your core. Beware of the root of bitterness forming in your root system. Your roots represent your relationship with yourself. Forgive and keep trusting God. Lack of forgiveness is like drinking poison, hoping the other guy dies. Keep your roots of mind and body clean and healthy by your choices. That way bitterness cannot take hold of you.

> *"A cheerful heart is good medicine, but a crushed*
> *spirit dries up the bones!"* —Proverbs 17:22, (NIV)

Again, all of us have mind stories that we are not always aware of, which are either supporting health or "taking us out" of health and success. That is why we must do as God tells us in the Bible to take every thought captive. Know what stories are going on for you. Are you running the "I can't, shouldn't or wouldn't" stories, or the "what if" story, or the "wish I would've, should've, could've" story?

We all have some of these stories. Learn to listen to your mind and brain talking to you. It is like the cartoon devil on one shoulder and the angel on the other.

Choose to say **out loud** to the devil on your shoulder, "Thank you, brain, for sharing, but STOP! I choose God's truth." **Choose** to listen to the angel on your other shoulder with Truth from Scripture in any given "story" situation. Choose to use "I am," "I can," or "I will" statements rather than "I'll try." **Try** is a powerless word and gives you permission to fail or not follow through. It "takes you out" and actually weakens your body. Have you ever heard never to "should" on yourself? The word "should" will weaken you physically, as will any word that is not a positive action statement. When speaking or singing, it is important to know the empowering words that make you feel in control and powerful versus weak. It is very important to know your passion and purpose, and speak and sing well with both in mind.

Identify your "stories" and choose to recreate positive truth-oriented ones. When I refer to truth, I always mean Biblically sound statements. I love it when scientists make statements that affirm Biblical truth. In fact, some say that if science does not agree with the Bible it is not sound science. Dr. Caroline Leaf, is one such scientist.[2]

The body needs the mind and brain for instruction and body chemistry. If you, as a speaker, are to think clearly and be healthy, you need your mind and brain input. Your brain can change your DNA. That means just because there is a dreaded disease in your family history, you can alter the situation with how you think! This is good news for sure!

Your body leg, or root system, needs your mind and brain leg, or root system, but the brain needs all the oxygen, water, exercise, nutrition, and rest (OWNER) elements of the body to stay healthy and functioning. Your spirit leg, or top of tree, gets its empowerment from the Holy Spirit of God and drives your thoughts, which drive the brain chemistry, which drives the body chemistry. But without the healthy body, the mind, and brain cease to exist. Without the mind and brain, the body ceases to exist. Your spirit needs your brain and body to exist on earth, so it can produce life-giving fruit and comforting shade for others. Your spirit lives on and carries your whole essence, either with God and heaven, or without Him to an unknown future when your body and brain die.

You want to be vibrant and healthy as a singer or speaker for obvious reasons. When you are vibrant and healthy, you have the thought, or idea capacity, and physical capacity to carry out all you've been called to do.

Also, the vocal cords need to be healthy, and need your spirit, mind and physical care and input. As stated in chapter 8, one can drink water and breathe steam from warm to hot liquids and water to help the cords perform well. There are a number of wives' tales about eating or drinking certain things for the voice. What I know for sure is that the vocal cords need to be hydrated, and water in your system is best for hydration. Drink at least one half your body weight in ounces of water daily. Keep sodas and carbonated liquids to a minimum. Menthol or peppermints are not good for vocal folds or cords, and reflux acid is also very damaging. Post nasal drainage also takes a toll on vocal folds or cords, so using antihistamines with expectorants may be helpful. Getting enough rest and eating smaller meals to avoid reflux is just good common sense when it comes to voice. Lemon in water is good, as it has an alkalizing effect on the body and thus vocal cords. Think belief in yourself and trust in God for your voice to stay open and strong.

When thinking of the power of the spirit, mind, and body connection, an amazing exercise to do is this: pray and ask God to show you something you believe He wants for you to do, have, or experience. Then write it out on one side of a ten-inch by twelve-inch by one-inch board. On the other side of the board write what you believe is holding you back. Now have two friends hold each side of the board, with the "what is holding you back" words facing you. Then with an appropriate stance (most dojo support can help you with this stance), proceed to break through the board to get to the other side of what it is you want. When you pray to God with your **spirit,** focus **mentally** on what you want but what is holding you back, and **physically** break through to what you want, you align every cell of your brain and body to your spiritual desire that is now effectively in God's hands. You cannot lose! I love to do this excercise with my workshop clients. It is amazing what happens.

At a men's church retreat, I took the men through this exercise. All but one large six-foot-two-inches tall man did the exercise. He was afraid of hurting his hand! I demonstrated and broke the board in front of all the men, and I am **not** a six-foot-two-inches tall large woman, but a five-foot-four-inches tall petite woman. He was allowing the **fear** to shut him down and keep him from a huge blessing.

Two weeks later, one of the men approached me to tell me how this had dramatically changed his life. He asked me if he could show me his broken board, and introduced his fiancée to me. What he wanted and prayed for that day as he physically broke through what he perceived was holding him back, was to be married. After the exercise, he was fully aligned with God, his spirit and prayer, his mind, and his body. Nothing was in his way any longer. His fiancée showed up for him because he was experiencing being **balanced** by the power of God working through his spirit, mind, and body at that moment.

I have done this several times and it is always thrilling. Is it scary? Yes. But that forces me to deal with that fear, take it captive, and **choose** to go for what I want by doing it anyway. Not only have I broken boards, but I have bent eight-foot rebar by holding it in my throat with a partner, praying, and having a very strong intention by the power of the Holy Spirit, walking toward my partner and watching that rebar bend in half!

Walking thirty-six feet of burning coals with a strong Biblically sound intention allowed me to walk with no sense of heat and no burns, while others were burned and hurt. My strong Biblical and spiritual intentions have been all about living my God-given purpose to be great at training and truly helping other people be their excellent best. Guess what? I cannot fail, because my "Three

Legged Stool" and my "Tree of Excellence" are all in alignment with God's truth, and He will not allow me to fail.

I will have moments of learning and stumbling, but I will not fall far or fail. I will only grow closer to Him through it all. There is a saying about entrepreneurs that failing is to be expected—just fail forward, don't stop. It is so true, and with God having your back, so-called failure is only a setback to be learned from on your journey forward to big wins. This knowledge helps you grasp the power and importance of the balance of the total you as demonstrated in the "Tree of Excellence" as a visual.

It Isn't How Hard You Fall, but Is How High You Bounce!

Your personality affects how you see the world around you. Be aware of self and look to mirror and understand the needs of the others in your life to accomplish a healthy and more balanced outlook. Remember, your purpose is also tied to you knowing yourself, what makes your heart sing, and how to use the good, bad, and in-between of life experience to truly bless others.

Being able to see balance in all these areas (spirit, mind, body and how that affects your personality, gifting, and all of you) is essential to you functioning healthily and well as a speaker or singer. The interdependence of all areas is real and necessary for you to be your awesome best!

Chapter 15

ALL TIED UP WITH A BOW

"For we are God's masterpiece. He has created us anew in Christ Jesus, so we can do the good things he planned for us long ago" — **Ephesians 2:10, (NLT)**

"For in him we live and move and have our being. As some of your own poets have said, 'We are his offspring.'" — **Acts 17:28, (NIV)**

Vocal Application: *This book is the owner's manual to your voice which is ALL of you. A recap of all the important parts of you and your voice is here in this chapter, plus a few new things. Your desire for excellence and your priorities in this life will determine how great a speaker or singer*

*you really are, even if you think you are hiding
them and fooling people. God created you for good
works, and as a speaker or singer, you have great
influence in the world. So be deliberate and careful
as to how you think and choose to act or carry out
your calling. Your success as a speaker depends
on your being true to who you really are, your priorities including God, and what you are called to
speak or sing about with expertise, vulnerability,
and excellence. Be determined to give your "special song" to the world. Don't die with the music of
your life still in you. Give it away! As the song says,
"Without a song the day would never end; without
a song the road will never bend; when things go
wrong, a man ain't got a friend, without a song...
I only know, there is no love at all without a song"
in your heart to share with others.*

Your authentic heart and passions show even when you think
you are camouflaging them, or are being intimidated out of
them. Be solid in who you are regardless of cultural influences. It
has been said that there are many "you's" depending on the situation. Like an actor who becomes different people on stage, you can
adapt and step up to the plate in any situation and be the **best you**
possible at that moment. But no matter the "you" that shows up,
grounded authenticity, heart, and passion must always be present.

I enjoyed the movie *God Is Not Dead*. It is a wonderful story
of a young college student who was not willing to be intimidated
by a professor of philosophy who wanted all his students to claim

and believe that God is dead. It shows how God used a faithful student whose love for God made a difference in the lives of many, including the professor, by his willingness to make a stand and challenge the professor's belief system in a kind and respectful way.

The bottom line of this book is that God is alive. He loves you and is for you. Just like the student and the professor in the movie, He created you with purpose and has a special unique job for you to do for Him in your ability to speak and sing. Communication is a gift from God to bless others. The student in the above mentioned movie really did bless the professor, because the professor admitted there is a God and that he was mad at Him for taking his mother too soon out of his life. The professor finally accepted Jesus as Savior, and the whole class of students had to really rethink what was true and not true through the whole story. The professor was angry at God and was influencing students negatively, but in the end he ended up blessing them with the gift of analyzing and thinking things through because of the Christ-believing student's convictions.

For you to know who you are, as discussed in chapters 1-3, it is critical in your knowing your voice, purpose, and success in this life. You are a spirit being living in a body with a brain and mind full of thoughts and emotions. So ask Jesus into your heart, and the Holy Spirit of God will meld with your spirit so that you can shine with brilliance in this world of speaking and singing. Then see how the Holy Spirit of God gives you brilliant messages full of His grace, love, and forgiveness. The world is a hurting place, and people need you and your unique special messages to free them to be all they can be.

You are like a puzzle piece, and there are people looking for you so that they can uniquely receive your message, and fit with you in order for their picture of life and who they are to be clearer.

Remember, you are like a tree whose core or trunk is Christ infused, with roots that go deep into the present culture. The picture of Jesus being the core vine in you, "The Tree of Excellence," and the tree top branches and root branches are pictured in Scripture.

> *"I am the vine; you are the branches. If you remain*
> *in me and I in you, you will bear much fruit; apart*
> *from me you can do nothing."* —John 15:5, (NIV)

As a "Tree of Excellence," you have mind and body roots to be cared for. These root systems represent your relationship with yourself. They are the source of nutrients carried in life-giving water to the leaves at the top of the tree where the powerful full spectrum "Son-light" transforms the root nutrients to life-giving energy, shade and fruit, which represent all the other relationships you have with God and other people. Be careful to monitor your attitudes and never allow a root of bitterness to develop and grow. It will destroy your healthy mind and body roots. By allowing the Son of God to be your core and your "Son-light," you are connected to God, and the Holy Spirit of God is melded with your spirit, giving you new insight and wisdom, thereby giving you the power of healthy choice in all your branches.

"I have come into the world as a light, so that no one who believes in me should stay in darkness." —John 12:46, (NIV)

A healthy life-giving spirit (connected to God's Spirit through Jesus) empowers you as the "Tree of Excellence," and creates your thinking patterns as you tune in to healthy life-giving truth to live by. By allowing God to be your best friend and guide, you ensure yourself of success in accomplishing your God-given purpose, which is the source of happiness in this life.

Just like the student who stood strong and passionately but respectfully against the professor's ideology, you can stand strong and passionately, and give your gifts to this world through your speaking. You can be all God wants you to be and do great things. Chapters 4 and 5 will help you with your understanding of Jesus and Spirit. I love what I heard once from an English evangelist. He said, "I am a Christian because it is true, I need forgiveness, Jesus bought me with His life on the cross to save and fix me, and Jesus is truly for all people."

Be careful what you allow into your mind roots through your five senses. What you watch, read, listen to, touch, smell, taste, and speak have the potential to either bless you and your passion and purpose or "take you out"! You must be diligent to develop healthy mind roots for healthy productive thinking.

"For as a man or woman thinks in the heart, so he or she is." —Proverbs 23:7, (NKJV)

217

"Always be full of joy in the Lord; I say it again, rejoice! Let everyone see that you are unselfish and considerate in all you do. Remember that the Lord is coming soon. Don't worry about anything; instead, pray about everything; tell God your needs and don't forget to thank him for his answers. If you do this, you will experience God's peace, which is far more wonderful than the human mind can understand. His peace will keep your thoughts and your hearts quiet and at rest as you trust in Christ Jesus." —Philippians 4:4-7, (TLB)

"Finally, brothers and sisters, whatever is true, whatever is noble, whatever is right, whatever is pure, whatever is lovely, whatever is admirable— if anything is excellent or praiseworthy—think on these things. 9 Whatever you have learned or received or heard from me, or seen in me—put it into practice. And the God of peace will be with you." —Philippians 4:8-9, (NIV)

Hope is said to equal "wishing" something would happen or change. Faith equals "believing" something will happen or change. Courage equals "making" something happen or change. When you speak, you use all your spirit, mind, and body, and you use hope, faith, and courage as well.

A quiet spirit sharpens perspective, purifies your heart, and clarifies your direction. Fear is a crippling emotion. What worries you, masters you. Courage is the quality of your mind and spirit that enables you to meet danger, opposition, or challenge of life with fearlessness, calmness, and firmness. Small fears become larger as you give attention to them.

See chapter 6 for more on the mind and how to release fear and dwell in faith and love.

"Knowing what must be done and taking action diminishes FEAR"—Rosa Parks.

Taking good care of your body with healthy oxygen, water, nutrition, exercise, and rest is paramount to building great body roots that feed your body, mind, and spirit in your "Tree of Excellence." It is difficult in the modern culture of sugars, smoke, and soda rather than water, but you can do it! Speaking or singing requires physical understanding of how the vocal systems work. There is much to be learned in chapters 7 and 8. Your voice is a triune system of vocal production, vocal support, and secrets of language creation, all fueled by you triune spirit, mind, and body.

There is power in the caress of safe loving touch and expression. You can strike out and create fear, or caress and create safety and love. Remember when speaking, the use of your hands as extensions of your arms and body moving space around you expresses your heart and authentic body energy as well. This and your total vocal systems are covered in chapter 8.

The technical side of voice is the easy part of this scenario, as discussed in chapter 8. Your three vocal system components of sound producing, sound supporting, and language skills are fun and relatively easy to master with the help and knowledge of the science and physiology of voice, which is my training passion. It is all these components and the rest of you that are the key to your success. Finding the "sweet spot" of your voice involves your thought management, your vocal horn, or pharynx management, and your body management, all beautifully coordinated and functioning in concert. So I cheer you on with a standing ovation from me to you! You were designed by God for brilliance and to have an awesome effect on all who know you and hear you.

Knowing how to be professional in your dress and total demeanor, as well as being healthy in body and mind, is critical to your speaking success. I see so many young women, in particular, who do not know how to dress for success in this modern world. Please read that chapter on the importance of and insights on your "wrapping." All is covered in chapter 9, including your stature, grounding, and much more.

Good etiquette is simply about honoring and respecting yourself and other people. When you speak or sing, be sure you dress one notch higher than your audience out of respect for them and yourself. They came to hear you, and in some cases, they paid good money to see and hear you. Please honor them and yourself by dressing appropriately so you can feel good about yourself and, more importantly, give of your best self without being self-conscious or worried about image. When you are relaxed about yourself and know that "nerves" are your best friend, you can be comfortable that God has your back, and you will deliver well what you came to say with excitement.

The power of your presence, engagement, your story, and analogous stories are in chapter 10. Your presence must be engaging, and you must understand and master the five important elements and incorporate them in your messages to anyone, anytime, anywhere. You possess much creativity from God, and He wants you to paint pictures with your words to engage and influence others for good. This chapter also shares some great engagement tools and video tips for effective videos. Most people are afraid of camera work, but it is truly a great medium when you know a few of these tricks.

Chapter 11 is all about understanding who you are as a personality with unique characteristics and psychological needs. Understanding yourself and being aware of and understanding the different personalities of others will give you an edge to being able to "get" them and give them what they need based on their psychological and emotional needs. As a speaker, these are golden keys to help you shine with loving brilliance. Knowing your personality and the unique way you think, process, and see the world is of utmost importance as a communicator. Even the loudness or quietness tendencies and emotion in your speaking voice are tied to your personality or temperament. Solutions of understanding lie here in this chapter.

A special new help for understanding the values and "buy"ology of others you are with is in chapter 12. The BANKcode methodology is all about values and why people buy into you or what you are sharing with them. Even when you know the psychologically based personality profile of someone, you can still step on their values and create communication challenges. In chapter 12, you discover the importance of quickly identifying the values and language of influence with a unique identity code of anyone you work or live with and the miraculous results that ensue when used. Your credibility depends on you understanding the truths shared in this chapter, and credibility is of ultimate importance for a speaker or singer.

Chapter 13 is all about your God-given purpose. Wow! In this chapter is a whole boatload of keys for you as a speaker or singer. Communication to an audience of one or many depends on you knowing yourself wholly. Your personality, your abilities, natural and spiritual gifting, the unique way you think, your heart, what makes it sing, and your experiences in life all become of prime importance when you want to be a great speaker or singer using the gift of your whole voice, which is the gift of **all** of you. Remember, knowing what to do takes you only so far; but knowing **why** you do what you do will always take you to the top. Your purpose is your **why** of life.

You and I are "cracked pots" and each crack hurts. Those cracks have the potential of victimizing you by your choice to be a victim, or choosing courage and let in God's light and perspective. God uses our cracks to enlighten us, order our steps, help us to see Him in the light, and grow. You can't grow and find your purpose without light. He calls us to be the light of the world by reflecting His great light to others. Speaking and singing are great light-giving activities and are much needed in our world.

Chapter 14 is all about creating balance with all of the areas in your life. Seeing yourself as the "Tree of Excellence" helps you see your time spent in relationship with God, yourself, and others, and the quality of your comforting shade, fruit bearing and giving. The quality of the fruit you produce coming through your voice to others has the power to bless and heal, or hurt and cause damage and destruction. Speaking uses the power of the tongue. There is power there to curse or bless, to heal or hurt. Scripture says it best when it says that God has laid it all before you, life, death, cursing, and blessing; choose life and blessing, and live. In the book of James, it cautions us about the untamable tongue and how to control it. Balance can only be achieved by being able to see it and work towards it. Even if you feel you are never truly in balance, by seeing it (as in the "Tree of Excellence") and working towards it, you actually stay in reasonable balance.

Bringing your mind into God's presence brings rest and renewal. You must have rest and renewal as a speaker. How can you hear from God if you are not spending time with Him? He infuses His thoughts into yours. As you do this, your mind stops racing, your body relaxes, and you become aware of God. That is such a huge blessing, and it really helps transform your tongue into a tool for good!

Meditation is a huge thing in our culture now, but God has said all along to meditate on Him and His Word day and night and experience His peace. *"Be still and know that I am God!"* Adam and Eve were designed for more than the dimensions we experience in time and space. The three space dimensions are height, width, and depth, with time being the fourth dimension.

There is at least one more dimension, and Adam and Eve accessed it. So can we. It is the key dimension of **openness to God's presence**, which transcends the others. This dimension gives you glimpses of heaven while still here on earth. Just choose to spend time calmly still and meditating on God and His truth. You will experience the difference of time, space, and openness to your Creator, your best friend in all the universe, God Himself. Even science now tells us that the spirit talks to the mind, which talks to the brain, which talks to the body. They all interact with each other as discussed in chapters 6 and 14. God Himself talks to us in our spirit, mind, brain, and body if we just get quiet with him and listen.

Shining with brilliance is knowing yourself wholly, spirit, mind, body, personality, and purpose. It is about knowing how to feed yourself well in mind and body, supporting your spirit. Remember, a powerful life-giving spirit only happens with the Holy Spirit of God connected and infused into your spirit, thus giving you a new mind, which in turn gives you a new healthy brain and body. Renewing your mind daily with truth from God's Word, the Bible, and great positive books feed your spirit, which feeds your mind, which changes brain chemistry, which changes body chemistry and leads to health. Choosing your thoughts and choosing to take good care of the body is essential to health. God's Spirit or "Son-shine" is the key to the miracle of life in you as a tree. It takes all three legs of your stool, or all three branch systems of you, the "Tree of Excellence," to be wholly healthy (spirit, mind, body) as seen in chapter 14 and this whole book.

Looking at your relationship with yourself in your roots, your tree-top fruit, and your use of time, as you engage all the tools I have shared with you, will help you thrive and make a difference for good in the lives of others.

I love what Zig Ziglar said that I have borrowed many times. "In any crowd, one in three people are either brilliant and beautiful, or highly attractive and very smart. Now look to your left and then your right. It clearly isn't them, so it must be You! If man can make penicillin out of moldy bread, just think what God, who created the universe, can do with you."

I agree with Zig and miss him now that he has gone on to heaven. But his legacy goes on and on because he was a great speaker who knew how to speak from the heart with passion and authentic desire to help his audiences. He used the English language well with no distracting "uhms" or extraneous words that expressed no purposeful meaning. He projected his message clearly and well through a great vocal instrument with plenty of his humorous personality. He used the contrast of fun and laughter with enough seriousness to get the message across and touch you with his complete presence. He clearly knew his purpose and executed it well through his "awesome" speaking and self. He was born to be awesome and so were you. Look to great examples like Zig for inspiration and quality.

Mentors matter

Zig Ziglar and Jean Lush, both have gone to be with Jesus in heaven, but they were great mentors to me through their writing and speaking. Joyce Landorf Heatherly, through her being "real" and all her writing, has influenced and mentored me. I have been blessed to know and be good friends with (as if a daughter) two beautiful and savvy women who are experts in professional dress, demeanor, and people skills. The first is Jerry Williamson. Jerry mentored me in fashion and knowing Jesus, a great combination. She spent most of her illustrious career as a gifted buyer in fashion retail for many years with a high-end group of boutiques. She produced multiple fashion shows for audiences of thousands over a number of years, in which I modeled and performed special music. She and I worked together in professional work and ministry for over twenty years, and she has always been a great inspiration to me. She encouraged me to go on with professional modeling and print work with prominent retailers, Nordstrom's and Bon Marche or Macy's being my favorites, but also with Microsoft and Franciscan Health in print work. I love her dearly, as she has always encouraged and loved me into my purpose. Jerry influenced my life and mentored me in such loving and guiding ways. I watched her and experienced her love, as she was a walking miracle and testimony to God's amazing grace and provision, complete with great real life stories of encounters with angels who helped her during strokes and other situations. God even took care to send an angel who showed up in white, opened the store entrance that was bolted with no key available, and then disappeared, all while others were watching. Through Jerry, God availed many miracles for myself and others to see and experience. My prayer has always been to be one tenth the mentor to others that she has been to me in our nearly fifty year relationship.

Second is Alma Gray-Martin, an amazing professional woman who has been a fabulous mentor to me. She is now one hundred and one years young (2017) and is still an amazing woman of inspiration to me. She is a writer, speaker, chaplain, and an active member of her community to this day. Alma dresses professionally and always represents class and confidence in her demeanor, but with love and compassion. She has been of great encouragement to me in my life and with this book. I love her for the great lady she is and for all her loving support to me over the nearly forty years I have had the privilege of knowing her.

Again, my prayer has always been to be as effective at blessing others as these two women have been for me. And to be great at communication and helping others as Zig, Jean, Joyce, and all my beloved mentors and trainers who have trained me and believed in me. Mentoring means believing more in the person in front of you than they do in themselves. Mentoring is a huge gift of helping others see themselves as capable and able to be and do all they were created to do and be. Mentors do matter hugely.

I have studied really great and successful speakers, singers, and actors for years as I have honed my own gifts and skills. It takes every piece of information I have shared in this book to help you see, understand, and experience true transformation into the awesome person God made you to be. Take on the challenge, and I will help you accomplish your desires through workshops and special training and coaching.

Believe me when I say, "You were truly born to be awesome and present and shine with brilliance through the awesome power of God in you, in any situation." I believe in you and trust Paul of Bible fame when he said:

> *"And I am certain that God, who began the good work within you, will continue his work until it is finished on the day when Christ Jesus returns." —* Philippians 1:6, (NLT)

> *"For I can do all things through Christ, who gives me strength." —* Phillipians 4:13, (NLT)

He **is** my strength. That scripture has helped me be strong in so many situations, I cannot count them all.

> *"Seek the Kingdom of God above all else, and live righteously, and he will give you everything you need." —* Matthew 6:33, (NLT)

> "... *The mind governed by the Spirit is life and peace*." — Romans 8:6 (NIV)

Believe in your heart and spirit. Use your mind to think and choose good thoughts by thinking about God's Word and application. Use your body by using your whole body and voice to speak truth and power of the Word out into existence. Use your amazing voice (all of you) to speak and sing all the awesomeness of you and your God-given messages into the world to bless and make it better.

Remember, you have everything you need to do a great job:

- Jesus and the Holy Spirit of God

- Sound mind with clarity of message with your mind map.

- Tall, grounded body in full health and stature with powerful vocal prowess.

- Love in your amazing expert's heart.

You Rock! Go, make it happen and bless your world because you truly are AWESOME!

Carol is available to bring joy to you and serve you with her radio show, *That Special Touch of God's Excellence* online at **KLAY1180.com** on Sunday afternoons from 2:00 to 3:00 PM, Pacific time. If you are in the Seattle area you can catch her live on air at 1180 on the AM dial. For archived shows, go to http:// www.voiceperformancecoach.com

CAROL L STANLEY

"Your passion, beauty within, and the impact you make can shine boldly on stage or camera from the inside out... if you just lean into it."

Voice Performance Coach and Presentation Skills Expert Carol Stanley guides church leaders, entrepreneurs, business professionals, and aspiring speakers and singers to gain confidence, poise, and command over voice, spirit, mind, and body. They transform from unsteady, shaky, and fearful to capable, confident, and compelling presenters who make big impact on audiences large and small, and on camera. Whether they speak or sing boldly or stand with power and impact without saying a word, these transformed presenters inspire, motivate, lead, and achieve to make the difference they are on the planet to make for the moments that matter the most.

Since 1974, Carol has guided hundreds of formerly frustrated clients to step into their own unique brand of stage brilliance. Beloved by many, she is known as the Fairy Godmother who sprinkles her special magic golden dust of presentation and voice skills to create golden outcomes in the balance sheet and beyond. She is a Premier Success Coach for EwomenNetwork, is recognized in Stanford's Who's Who and Continental Who's Who, and has been published and recognized as a business leader in *Women of Distinction* magazine. Carol is a published author of the book, *Incredible Life*, and of her newest book, *Born to Be Awesome*: *A Guide to Presenting with Brilliance on Stage and Camera Through the Power of God in You.*

Carol comes to her gift and talent to make others stars in their own lives and businesses from her own career on stage and screen. Carol has modeled fashion clothing on the Seattle-area runways for Nordstrom, Macy's, Penny's, and others, and performed in movies, television, and stage performances including a regular on TBN TV "Seattle Praise The Lord," KOMO TV "Northwest Afternoon," and other guest spots. She has performed female leads in the musical productions of *Music Man, King and I, Li'l Abner, Pirates of Penzance, Wizard of Oz,* and others. She has written and directed choral and dramatic musical stage productions, and recorded music albums as well. As a result, Carol knows the landscape to guide clients to succeed with poise, grace, and ease to make the most of their time to shine.

Whether working one-on-one with action-taking clients or leading her popular workshops, one thing is certain. Clients rave about the impact Carol delivers in service to their big success.

Book Carol L. Stanley for your next big event.

Whether Carol is addressing an intimate group or a standing-room-only crowd, count on Inspirational Speaker, Carol Stanley, to inspire audience members to embrace great vocal and communication skills, and push past their fears to shine brilliantly in service to others. She is a crowd-pleasing, life-changing speaker, and break-out session leader who adds massive value with every innovative and income increasing speaking strategy she shares.

Please feel free to contact Carol at the following:
carol@voiceperformancecoach.com

Go to: http://voiceperformancecoach.com
to sign up for a free gift and
schedule a time to talk to Carol
253–951–3879 text or call

"No eye has seen, nor ear has heard, and no mind has imagined what God has prepared for you, who love him." —1 Corinthians 2:9, (NLT)

BIBLIOGRAPHY

[1] Dr. Leaf, Caroline, *Who Switched Off My Brain, Controlling Toxic Thoughts and Emotions*. Nashville, TN: Thomas Nelson, 2009, *www.harpercollinschristian.com*.

[2] Dr. Leaf, Caroline, *Switch On Your Brain, The Key to Peak Happiness, Thinking and Health*. Grand Rapids, MI: Baker Books, 2013, *www.bakerbooks.com*.

[3] Dr. Oz, Mehmet, *You On A Diet*. 1230 Avenue of the Americas, New York, NY, 10020: Free Press, a division of Simon & Schuster, Inc., 2006, 2009, *www.simonandschuster.com*.

[3] Dr. Davis, William, *Wheat Belly Total Health*, Emmaus, Pennsylvania, New York, NY, Rodale Books, 2014.

*Herbals Carol takes for help with asthma: Phytocort and Resprin. Both can be purchased at www.betterhealthinternational.com

[4] Rush, Callan, *Wealth Through Workshops*, www.callanrush.com, www.lucrativeliminarytraining.com.

[5] Dr. Keis, Ken, *Why Aren't You More Like Me?*, *Discover the Secrets to Understanding Yourself and Others*. Abbotsford, BC Canada: CRG Publishing, 2011, *http://www.crgleader.com/about-crg-team-assessments-training.html*
Contact Carol for special pricing, 253-951-3879, or email, carol@voiceperformancecoach.com

[6] Tree, Cheri, *Why They Buy*, www.BANKcode.com
Use code, CLStanley for pricing advantage